BE YOUR BEST
PRESENTER
. . . AND BEYOND

Alan Mars

Q·LEARNING

For UK orders: please contact Bookpoint Ltd, 130 Milton Park, Abingdon, Oxon OX14 4SB.
Telephone: +44 (0) 1235 827720. Fax: +44 (0) 1235 400454. Lines are open 09.00–18.00, Monday to Saturday, with a 24-hour message answering service. You can also order through our website www.madaboutbooks.co.uk

British Library Cataloguing in Publication Data A catalogue record for this title is available from The British Library.

This edition, first published in UK 2003 by Hodder Headline Plc, 338 Euston Road, London NW1 3BH

Typeset by Servis Filmsetting Ltd, Manchester, England
Printed in Great Britain for Hodder & Stoughton Educational, a Division of Hodder Headline Plc, 338 Euston Road, London NW1 3BH by Cox & Wyman Ltd, Reading, Berkshire.

Impression number   10 9 8 7 6 5 4 3 2 1
Year   2007 2006 2005 2004 2003

Contents

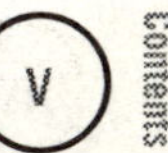

v

Series Introduction

Perhaps you have had an idea, or wanted to achieve something, but known that you not only need some skills but also help with taking the risk and doing it for real. Maybe you have thought 'it is easy for him/her but not for me . . .'

This series is written for people who haven't got the time (or money) to attend a long training course or who are not lucky enough to be managed and mentored by a star in the field in which they want to succeed. These books will be 'back pocket' resources that will inspire and give practical tips that you can read up on and use in the next few minutes. They will also help you feel confident in taking skills that you already have into new situations at work, home and the community.

Lesley Gosling
Q. Learning

Introduction

THESE SHOES WERE MADE FOR TALKIN'

The late Dirk Bogarde found that when he got the right pair of shoes that fitted the personality of the character he was playing, everything else fell into place.

Surely there is more to performing than finding the right pair of shoes? Yes, of course there is, but for Dirk Bogarde the totality of his acting experience somehow became anchored to the shoes.

The information and exercises in this book come from my own 20 years' experience as a presenter and from numerous other sources. I have my own pair of shoes. They are fairly flexible and, as an interim measure, have fitted a lot of people. You are welcome to try them and walk in them for a while. However, with increasing practise and experience, I am confident that you will find your own pair of shoes . . .

CHAPTER 1
What if I Were a Better Presenter?

> All the world's a stage
> And all the men and women merely players.
>
> SHAKESPEARE – AS YOU LIKE IT

> All the world's a stage and most of us are desperately unrehearsed.
>
> SEAN O'CASEY

WHAT WOULD MAKE ME BETTER?

Imagine for a moment what it would be like if you were a better presenter. What would you see in your not-too-distant future? Would you, perhaps, have more of that confidence and composure that is so desirable and so enviable in others? Don't you love it when the skilled performer in any field makes it all look so effortless, so natural?

Perhaps you are already a good presenter. But what if you could have those qualities even more reliably, stronger and for longer? How would it affect your confidence and your personal presence? How would it affect you professionally and personally? More job satisfaction? More money? Exciting challenges?

2500 YEARS OF THEATRE

The roots of our present theatrical tradition stretch back 2500 years to its origins in classical Greek theatre and oratory. Every time you go to the theatre or cinema or simply watch adverts on the television you will be watching actors using techniques drawn from this ancient tradition. Since those times, and before, performers have used a wide variety of techniques to propel them into a resourceful state of mind, body and voice from which to give an impactful performance.

The chapters which follow present a number of techniques drawn from the performing arts and a variety of other sources. These techniques are specifically tailored for use in a wide variety of business contexts: presentation and communication skills; coaching skills; leadership training; influencing others with integrity; dealing with challenging people and challenging situations.

ANCHORING

One of the most important presentation techniques is **anchoring**. An anchor is a device for stabilizing a sailing vessel, large or small, in a potentially unstable and stormy medium, the sea. In performance terms an anchor is a specific stimulus that stabilizes certain conditions of body and mind in the potentially unstable and stormy medium called life. This is often done unconsciously in the form of various lucky charms.

Luciano Pavarotti, opera singer:

> When I perform in concerts, I use certain tricks that make me feel more secure. Everybody knows about my white handkerchief, which I used in my first concert in Missouri in 1973, in case I started to perspire. I find that I feel much better if I have it out there with me. It has a function but it's also for good luck.

> **Jack Welch,** chief executive of General Electric 1981–2001:
>
> For the past 24 years, I have had a lucky charm — a brown leather briefcase — that has come with me everywhere. My assistant Roseanne nicknamed it 'Mr Lucky'. I won the briefcase in an Atlanta golf tournament in 1977. It has seen better days. It's battered and bruised or, as Roseanne likes to say, 'It's disgusting and looks diseased!' I've done extremely well with Mr Lucky. It's been good to me, and I never wanted to give it up.

So how is it possible to take these external lucky charms and internalize them? How can a lucky charm transform from haphazard luck to a regular, reliable resource?

THE WISDOM OF INSECURITY

Performing artists can help you with confidence and vocal and physical presence, but that is where any similarity between business and theatre work ends . . . isn't it? Actually, the similarities between mainstream business and the performing arts are increasing all the time. Until 15 years ago a skilled and conscientious worker could reasonably expect to spend decades, if not their whole working life, in a given job. Nowadays short-term contracts are increasingly popular. To spend as much as ten years in one company is the exception rather than the rule. Jack Welch recognizes this reality and puts an extremely positive frame around it:

Any organization that thinks it can guarantee job security is going down a dead end. Only satisfied customers can give people job security. Not companies. That reality put an end to the implicit contracts that corporations once had with their employees . . . The psychological contract had to change. I wanted to create a new contract, making GE jobs the best in the world for people willing to compete. If they signed up, we'd give them the best training and development and an environment that provided plenty of opportunities for personal and professional growth. We'd do everything to give them the skills of 'lifetime employability', even if we couldn't guarantee them 'lifetime employment'.

The world of the performing arts, on the other hand, has always been insecure. The majority of skilled and talented artists live a rather precarious financial existence. Successful performing artists become adept at consciously developing a sense of inner security and confidence that persists regardless of external circumstances. Or, as the veteran British comedian **Bob Monkhouse** puts it:

And the moral is: if you're a superstitious person and derive comfort from some lucky mascot, keep it with you — but don't depend on it so much that its loss will weaken your self assurance. There's only one charm you should rely on — your own.

If you want a lifetime of employability and more then make sure that your lucky charm lives with you, in your centre, at all times. To find out how, read on . . .

TOOLS FOR YOUR JOURNEY

In eating a cake some ingredients are virtually invisible to the naked tongue — the egg, for example. The fruit, nuts, icing or cherry on top will be the ingredients that make your mouth water, but you would certainly notice if the egg was not there as the whole cake would run the risk of falling apart. The egg does a fantastic job of blending diverse ingredients together into a palatable, delicious whole. And, amongst the whole variety of tantalizingly different cakes, certain ingredients crop up again and again.

There are no new ingredients in this book but there are some new combinations of ingredients (theories and practical exercises) and some unique flavours (the voices of those who have achieved great things) to inspire and motivate you. Enjoy.

Eyes and ears

For people living busy lives there is so much going on that, just to get from A to B, it seems necessary to screen out most distractions. The next time you are travelling during rush hour pause for a moment and wake up. Look around you. How many other people are truly awake? How many are frowning and chewing over thoughts unrelated to the present moment? How many have a good awareness of what is going on all around them? And how many have tunnel vision? The ability to chew over past and future and to narrow down attention on to specific goals is a great blessing and uniquely human.

Terry Pratchett, a best-selling British author, can always be relied upon for a fresh and humorous take on most subjects:

> People have reality dampers. It is a popular fact that nine-tenths of the brain is not used and, like most popular facts, it is wrong. The brain is used. And one of its functions is to make the miraculous seem ordinary and turn the ordinary into the usual.
>
> Because if this was not the case, then human beings, faced with the wonderousness of everything, would go around wearing big stupid grins . . . Part of the brain exists to stop this happening. It is very efficient. It can

 make people experience boredom in the middle of marvels.

Wake up and use your eyes and ears. The world is full of the most marvellous examples of communication and presentation skills. And if you don't already have them yourself . . . steal them! The wonderful thing about behavioural theft is that you can enrich yourself without impoverishing anyone else.

GETTING STARTED

How do you approach a book? Are you a 'skimmer', a 'dipper', a 'beginning to ender'? Do you prefer information or practical exercises? Do you go for text or graphics? All these learning styles, or any mixture of them, can be accommodated within this book.

You, the amateur or professional, a new or experienced communicator, will learn how to get into an optimum physical and mental state for making your presentation. Human beings are intrinsically gregarious creatures and, given the best contexts for development, they grow into naturally excellent communicators. However, not all of us have been graced with the best contexts for development – and this is where the value of the exercises comes in.

Many of the exercises in this book are **subtractive**. They involve a process of letting go of the habits that hinder easy expression. Other exercises are **additive**. They plant a seed that grows and develops over the course of time.

TERMINOLOGY

The word **presenter** is used throughout in a general way, from business, education, community and anyone else involved in the business of communication to small, large, formal or informal groups. The words **audience** or **listeners** refer to classes, trainees, teams, clients etc.

The word **kinaesthetic** refers to the internal body sense which gives you messages about levels of tension and relaxation, your posture, the position of your body in space and the relative sense of effort or ease that you experience in any given activity.

STARTING THE WORK

Some people will prefer to work through each exercise in sequence while others will prefer to read the whole book first to become familiar with the thinking behind it. Either approach is legitimate. Some sections of the book may seem more appropriate to your needs than others. You may wish to focus on a select few exercises for some time before moving on. Keeping a journal in which you note down brief details of how the work is progressing can be very helpful.

Loosen tight or uncomfortable clothing so that you can breathe and move more freely. A real luxury would be to work with a friend or colleague and guide each other through an exercise. It is also possible to read an entire exercise a few times, silently or aloud, and then refer to the instructions periodically as you go along. Take enough time to approach the exercises in a calm and unhurried way. If you have only ten minutes to spare, try working with a smaller chunk of a longer exercise. If you have any degree of physical disability, you can easily adapt all the exercises to suit your particular situation.

Materials

A hand-held tape recorder is an inexpensive and portable way of getting unbiased feedback about your presentations. You will also need one or two full-length mirrors in which to observe yourself while carrying out some of the exercises.

A POSITIVE ATTITUDE

Remember – seriousness, grim determination and striving for results are counter-productive. The qualities that will enhance your work and speed up your progress are:

- humour
- curiosity
- patience
- a playful attitude.

The changes that you make in any one session will usually be fairly small, but if you work in an easy and consistent way you will be surprised at how quickly they accumulate.

If, during the exercises, you find that your attention and actions are parting company, pause for a moment or two and gently let them come back together again. If your mind keeps wandering, stop the exercise and come back to it later. Two minutes of easy work is better than an hour of frowning concentration. Enjoyment is the key to continuing motivation.

CHAPTER 2
What Does Better Look Like?

Presence: The quality of self-assurance and effectiveness that permits a performer to achieve a rapport with the audience: stage presence.

AMERICN HERITAGE DICTIONARY OF THE
ENGLISH LANGUAGE

STYLE

Today there is enormous scope for personal style in the world of presentation. It is fantastic when you get things right by instinct, but instinct is often an unreliable ally. Training and application, however, substitute extremely well for instinct. In fact, with sufficient repetition some aspects of training become extremely efficient and streamlined. They turn into an unconscious competence – a learned instinct. This frees up your conscious awareness for other things and enhances your flexibility and fluidity as a presenter.

Progress now

As a first step towards unconscious competence, you need to identify some of the answers to these questions:

- What does a compelling presenter look like?
- What do they sound like?
- How do they make you feel?

The responses often take the following form: 'A compelling presenter is confident, assured, has authority, relates to the audience etc.'

But confident, assured and authoritative may mean something slightly different to each person. Now use your eyes and ears to answer these questions:

How does confidence stand? _______________________________

How does confidence walk? _______________________________

How does confidence look the audience in the eye?

____

At what pace and pitch does confidence speak?

____

THE SINGER AND THE SONG

Robin Prior, co-author of *NLP and the New Bazaar*, a guide to sales training, says that there are two aspects to any presentation – the **song** and the **singer**, i.e. what you say and how you say it. The 'what' consists of the words and language and the 'how' consists of body language and the voice.

Research by **Albert Merhabian** suggests that people pay relatively little attention to what you say (as little as 7 per cent) and more to how you say it (as much as 93 per cent). This '93 per cent factor' is composed largely of the presenter's visual impact – posture, movement, gesture – and their voice – tone, pitch, flexibility and volume.

Even acknowledged experts in their fields lose their audience's attention through poor vocal and physical presentation – anything from a nervous, jarring delivery to a boring, monotonous one, accompanied by a matching style of body language which rapidly communicates the discomfort of the speaker to the audience.

ALIVE RELAXATION

Other speakers have the enviable ability to maintain a state of **alive relaxation** during their presentations. This is communicated to the audience by the way in which the speaker stands and moves, and through the flexibility and tone of their voice. This, in turn, increases the audience's attention level and ensures that the presenter actually manages to get the message across.

For many people the 93 per cent factor can seem frustratingly out of reach. But developing this quality of alive relaxation is not as difficult as it appears. A good start to changing this state of affairs is to develop a much clearer idea of what alive relaxation in presentation looks like, sounds like and feels like.

Progress now

Observe family, friends and colleagues as they interact. When do they peak? What happens physically and vocally?

VITAL INGREDIENTS FOR THE COMMUNICATION CAKE

What a delicious cake! But what are the ingredients? How is it made?

There are three piles of ingredients — a huge pile, a medium pile and a small pile: the **visual**, the **vocal** and the **verbal**. Each is full of a tantalizing variety of delicious ingredients:

VISUAL — Presenter's body language:

- Stature
- Head-neck-shoulder relationship
- Facial expression
- Eye contact
- Gestures
- Stillness/movement
- Owning space
- Proximity

AUDITORY – Presenter's voice:

- Volume/resonance
- Pace, rhythm and articulation
- Pitch and variation
- Silence and pause

VERBAL – Presenter's language:

- Structure and sequence
- Accessibility – clear English etc.
- Engagement – stories, metaphors, analogies
- Individuality – sensory words

Although the words comprise the smallest pile in the cake mix, they impart incredible flavour to the final product. By managing the physical and vocal aspects of your presentation skilfully a door will be opened. This door gives your audience access to your words and to the message that they convey. This door is called **rapport**.

OBSERVATION AND FEEDBACK — VISUAL, VOCAL AND VERBAL

One of the benefits of attending a course on presentation skills is to get skilful support and feedback from the course facilitator. Feedback from other members of the group can also be very useful if it is done constructively. In the absence of a presentation skills course you can use television, radio and, finally, real life to assess what you find compelling, or otherwise, in the way that people communicate. Start by focusing on the visual. Then move on to the vocal. And finally move onto the verbal.

Visual

Watch a television programme with the sound turned down. Make notes about the presenter or actor's body language:

ℹ	Posture ____

ℹ	Head-neck-shoulder relationship ____________________

ℹ	Facial expression _________________________________

- Eye contact ____
- Gestures ____
- Stillness/movement ____________________________________
- Owning space ____
- Proximity to others ___________________________________

Turn to programmes you wouldn't normally watch — the body language may well be quite different.

If you are feeling adventurous, copy some of the body language. If you can copy it you are almost certainly seeing it clearly.

Vocal

Listen to the television with the sound on and your eyes closed. Try copying how the presenter is speaking. Don't worry if you don't actually sound like the person you are copying. The purpose of the copying is to make you listen to the voice of the presenter or actor. Now make notes on their voice:

- Volume ____

- Pace and rhythm ___________________________________

- Articulation _______________________________________

- Pitch and variation ________________________________

- Resonance ____

- Silence and pause __________________________________

Every now and then open your eyes and check to see how much the voice and the body language match or mismatch each other.

Listen to the radio, especially talk-intensive programmes. Is there a difference between radio and television delivery?

Verbal

Finally, bring the words into the equation by analysing them in this way:

- Accessibility – simple, clear language ___________________
- Structure and sequence of the subject ___________________
- Use of stories, metaphors and analogies ___________________
- Sensory words:
  - visual, auditory and feeling words ___________________
  - words describing taste and smell ___________________

Can you think of a presenter who has a good balance of all three? Keep your eyes and ears open and enjoy the variety and richness around you.

WHO ARE YOUR FAVOURITE PRESENTERS?

There are an absolute host of them out there. Excellent role models come from every walk of life – work, community, media, theatre, politics, friends and family. What is it they do that grabs your attention? Do these role models engage other people's attention to the same degree that they engage yours? Just how common is it to find an excellent model of communication and presentation skills?

Many people are in the position of having to deliver set presentations. While this may be restricting from one point of view, from another it can be quite liberating. As long as the set presentation is of a sufficiently good quality and in line with your beliefs and values it can be a platform from which to explore the more performance-related, non-verbal aspects of presentation. After all, most actors and singers spend the majority of their performing career using other people's words, mostly to very good effect.

YOUR OWN RADIO REPORT

So, who is your favourite presenter? In this exercise you will become a radio reporter who is bringing their favourite presenter to life in the minds of their listeners. Having a tape recorder to speak into is not essential but it helps many people to get into character. Remember, this is not live radio. It doesn't have to be perfect. It can either be edited later or you can have several attempts until you feel satisfied.

Progress now

1   Think of someone who is a good presenter. They can be from as broad a category as you like – work, television, theatre, social or family. It could refer to formal or informal presentations.

2   When you are with this person, what do you see? Describe this out loud into your tape recorder. Paint as vivid a word picture as possible – remember that it is going to be broadcast to radio listeners nationwide.

3   Start with the most basic information first – the name of your presenter and your relationship to them, for example:

Hello. I would like to introduce you to my favourite presenter. His/her name is _____________ and he/she is (my boss, cousin, colleague, a well-known star of stage and screen . . .)

4 Now describe your presenter in the most basic terms – height, age, gender, how they dress etc:

Janet/John is about ＿＿＿＿＿ tall . . .

5 How do they sit, stand or move when they are speaking. What is their eye contact like?

Janet/John moves about quite a lot while presenting and every now and then when he/she really wants to make an important point he/she stands very still and holds your gaze for a long time . . .

6 What do you hear? How do they speak – fast/slow; high/low?

He/she speaks quietly but audibly with lots of variation . . .

7 What kind of language or speech do they use?

Janet speaks very simply and to the point, without being patronizing; John is a real storyteller, often going off at tangents and bringing the strands together at the end . . .

8 Having brought your presenter to life in the minds of your listeners go on to tell them a bit more about why you find the presenter so compelling. If some of their magic could rub off onto you, what would it be?

9 **Conclude your presentation:**

And that was my favourite presenter, Janet/John Smith. Thank you and goodbye from me, your roving reporter ＿＿＿＿＿. Tune in again next week for the next exciting episode.

Maria works for a large financial institution. She was eager to forward her career as much as possible over the next few years. She came to me for training because she had a tendency to race ahead in her speech. She wanted to become calmer and more authoritative through pacing her speech more effectively.

To help Maria do this, we worked on a Shakespeare sonnet that not only helped her to slow down but also to speak with a fuller and more resonant quality. We recorded each recitation then did some exercises. After this we would go through the process of reciting, recording and listening again. Maria's use of her voice gradually improved with each successive repetition.

The radio reporter exercise described above really seemed to bring together all the previous strands that we had been working on.

When Maria started to describe her favourite presenter, she began to use strong, powerful gestures and a more measured, confident voice. She eliminated the hesitant gestures that can often be seen as the visual equivalent of tripping over or struggling to find the right words.

Maria recited her sonnet once again. It had improved a lot. Some of the qualities that she found so appealing in her chosen presenter had spontaneously been incorporated into her body language and voice.

Progress now

This is an exercise you can try anywhere. It utilises your mind's eye, your mind's ears and your immediate responses. But be careful – if you do this in a public place some of the results could make you laugh out loud and could attract some alarmed or concerned glances from those around you.

1   Take a moment to think about your body. Get as close to a pleasantly neutral physical and mental place as possible. Let go of any unnecessary tension – put your bag between your feet if you are standing. Make sure your weight is evenly distributed between your left and right feet if you are standing and between your left and right buttocks if you are sitting.

2   Now use your mind's ear to conjure up a voice with the quality of nails dragging down a blackboard – a grating sound. Having noticed your physical and other responses to that voice, return to your pleasantly neutral state.

3   Repeat the same procedure for a number of other voices:

- boring
- clear but fairly neutral
- sexy
- authoritative
- passionate and engaging.

You may find that as you get a voice in your mind's ear, an image of a particular person will pop up to accompany it.

4   Now do this exercise the other way around. Conjure up images in your mind's eye of the qualities above then think about the voice.

DELIVERY

For any script, text or presentation, a wide range of deliveries is possible — from the uncomfortable (for both speaker and listener) to the compelling and engaging.

You may recall the actor **Peter Sellers** performing a spoken rendition of the Beatles song *A Hard Day's Night* dressed in Elizabethan costume. He delivered it in a serious, declamatory, mock-Shakespearean style which had its intended effect — incongruous and comedic. Under most circumstances you will want to be as congruent as possible when presenting, with body, voice, feeling and message all knitting together. But the very incongruity of comedy can highlight beautifully those qualities that bring engagement and rapport to a presentation.

Progress now

Take some of the voices above – grating, boring, clear but fairly neutral, sexy, authoritative, passionate and engaging. Imagine them reading the nursery rhyme below. Try reading it out loud in each type of voice.

Oh, the Grand Old Duke of York,

He had ten thousand men.

He marched them up to the top of the hill

And he marched them down again!

And when they were up they were up

And when they were down they were down.

And when they were only half way up

They were neither up nor down.

LISTEN AND LEARN

When you next listen to a presentation, analyse the constituent elements that make up that person's voice (you could do the same with their body language). You will soon start to realize why you respond to different speakers in different ways. If a grating voice, for example, creates tension in you, it is likely that the speaker is, at that moment at least, also experiencing stress on some level. What about the quiet authority of a particular newsreader's voice? You will also see that reflected in their physical demeanour. In the course of daily life, become more sensitive to the variety of voices around you. Keep your eyes open, too – does a person's body language and voice seem to match or mismatch?

THE HOME HAM-LET

A quick word on the subject of time and practice — people who have busy professional and home lives often complain that they have no opportunities to practise voice work. In fact, if you have young children you have a wonderful opportunity to practise. When you read them a story, bring some of your vocal qualities into the voices of the different characters. Ham it up a bit. Exaggerate. Ninety-nine times out of a hundred they will absolutely love it . . . and love you. And that is exactly what most presentations are about — winning the love of the really important few.

If you don't have children to practise with, recite some nursery rhymes or children's stories to a willing listener who has a high tolerance for eccentric behaviour.

ROBIN PRIOR

Robin Prior is a writer and performance skills trainer for business and the arts

RP: The great presenters are people who are totally in the subject. With some presenters it's like 'I'm the presenter. This is the subject. We are separate. So if you don't like the subject you can still like me.' The compelling presenters are those people who are totally committed to it, totally inside it, don't want to be separated from it. It is almost as if the subject starts in the middle of them, at their centre of gravity, and then radiates out, like those ornaments where if you touch the side the electrical force sparks out and comes to meet your finger.

A great example of this commitment is **Billy Connolly**, because he is 100 per cent present. He takes a risk because he doesn't have a script – he just has some subjects that he works with. And he takes it on trust that he is going to do it and it happens. You never get a sense with Billy Connolly that he is delivering material. He is there with you in a way that a really good presenter never just delivers material.

I think he is a genius at communicating. There are obviously going to be other parts of him that you don't see but you get this strong sense when you see him that you are getting Billy Connolly and not a stage persona. Total commitment, 100 per cent doing, 100 per cent there, not holding back.

What I get from someone like Billy Connolly is that they are giving me all that they can give me. I find that very respectful. If I am working with a group of people, I'm not there just because they are paying me lots of money. These people have committed time to this so it is only respectful for me to give them everything while I am there. I am committed to their outcomes, for that presentation.

AM: So there is none of 'I'll hold this back for stage two, for the second course'?

RP: There is only so much content you can handle. There is certain amount that people will learn at any given time and it is different for different people. And you have to gauge that by looking at their response rates and attention. But whatever you do with content, you must apply yourself to it 100 per cent.

CHAPTER 3

Creating a Compelling Goal

I am the most spontaneous speaker in the world because every word, every gesture and every retort has been carefully rehearsed.

GEORGE BERNARD SHAW

Imagination is the beginning of creation.

GEORGE BERNARD SHAW

THROUGH POISE TO PURPOSE

She stands in the middle of the room, gazing through the plate glass windows. She is standing in an easily upright manner, weight distributed, head balanced, shoulders easy and wide. She is dressed in smart business attire. Her name is Celia. On closer inspection her eyes are somewhat unfocused. She is, apparently, talking out loud to herself. She is giving a rich verbal description of someone, also called Celia, who is giving an excellent presentation:

Celia pauses briefly. She is physically and emotionally composing herself, before she enters the room. She's ready now. Celia enters the room and stands at her full height and width. She smiles at the group of people and says, 'Good morning everyone!' in a clear, ringing voice. She's certainly got everybody's attention as she walks up to the podium. She is now taking a moment to calmly sort out her notes. She puts the notes down, looks up and makes warm eye contact with people on the left, on the right and then in the middle of her audience. She is now saying, 'Good morning.

My name is Celia Wallace' to the left of the audience; 'I am a manager from Human Resources' while looking to the right of the audience; 'and today I am going to talk to you about our team strategy for next year' as she looks to the middle.

Should we be alarmed at this unusual behaviour? Seek urgent medical advice?

Celia is practising a technique beloved of sports psychologists that gives athletes a leg-up into the peak performance zone. She is talking her performance through from a third person perspective. This detached perspective allows her to imagine herself giving the presentation her best possible shot. It helps her to reduce her habitual feelings of panic at the prospect of giving a presentation.

Many professional sports teams employ sports psychologists who use a variety of techniques to help the team members to improve their performance. At the forefront of these techniques are procedures that harness the power of the imagination.

Such techniques were studied by a psychologist called **Alan Richardson**. A group of subjects received coaching in how to take free throws at a basketball basket. They were then split into three separate groups. Group one was instructed to practise free throws for 20 minutes per day. Group two visualized doing free throws for 20 minutes per day. The third group did no practice at all. The results at the end of 20 days were surprising. The 'real' practice group improved by 24 per cent. The visualization group improved by 23 per cent. The third group, unsurprisingly, did not improve at all.

The imagination has no bar to perfection. There is nothing to stop the least skilled player from imagining themselves engaging in sporting or, in your case, presentational feats of the highest level of skill. While this does not automatically guarantee that you will become a world class presenter or sports personality, it does provide a way in which you can rise into your peak performance zone.

THE VMBR STUDIES

In another study **Dr Richard Suinn** of Colorado State University developed a method called **visio-motor behaviour rehearsal (VMBR)**. This combines deep muscle relaxation exercises with mental imaging of the skill that is being learned.

In one study a group of 32 new karate students was divided into four groups. Each student underwent an anxiety and skills test, then each group was given a different home practice to do over the following six weeks:

- Group 1: Deep muscle relaxation only
- Group 2: Imaging only – visualizing the karate techniques in the mind's eye
- Group 3: VMBR – relaxation exercises followed by visualization
- Group 4: No home practice of any description.

At the end of the six-week period the students were again given anxiety tests. They were also given a traditional karate grading test. The VMBR and relaxation-only group both recorded lower levels of anxiety than the other groups. In the sparring tests the VMBR group demonstrated a clear superiority.

The same method that can help a karate practitioner to reduce anxiety and increase skill for the purposes of examination can be used to help you, the presenter, increase your verbal and non-verbal composure and reduce your anxiety at the prospect of presenting.

AN INTRODUCTION TO ALIVE RELAXATION

The karate-based study above says it all — most presenters want to be able to reduce their anxiety and improve their performance.

'Personal presence' depends on the practice of surprisingly simple yet fundamental skills. The exercises that follow are similar to those that an actor would use to prepare voice and body for going on stage.

In this section you will be exploring the physiology of confidence by visiting a number of physical landmarks on your own body:

- Your centre of gravity
- Your feet and how your body weight drops through them into the ground
- Peripheral vision and your sense of personal space.

Having familiarized yourself with these physical landmarks of confidence you will find it very easy to practise them. If you ever have to wait — in shops, at traffic lights, for tickets — instead of getting bored or frustrated you will now be able to practise and reinforce your new strategies.

YOUR CENTRE OF GRAVITY

In 1681 a Neapolitan mathematician, Giovanni Borelli, made a novel use of a see-saw to determine the centre of gravity of the human body. He made one person lie flat across the see-saw. The see-saw would become evenly balanced only when the person had their full weight equally distributed on either side of the pivot. Borelli determined from this that the centre of gravity was located between the buttocks and the pubic bone, just in front of the sacrum — the wide, wedge-shaped bone that comprises the base of the spine.

This principle applies when standing, too. When you are balanced the weight of your whole body is evenly distributed, from left to right, from front to back, from the very top of the head, through the centre of gravity and all the way down to the soles of your feet. The shoulders sit easily on either side of this gravity line. The statues from the archaic period of ancient Greece are like this — beautifully poised, upright and balanced — and consequently require very small plinths to prevent them toppling. Statues of the later periods are more asymmetrical and unbalanced from front to back. They require huge plinths and other props to stop them from falling over. Human beings do not have plinths; we rely on muscular tension to stop us from falling over when we are out of balance. We have to take responsibility for our own co-ordination and balance. Being psychologically balanced and centred is intimately related to being physically balanced and centred.

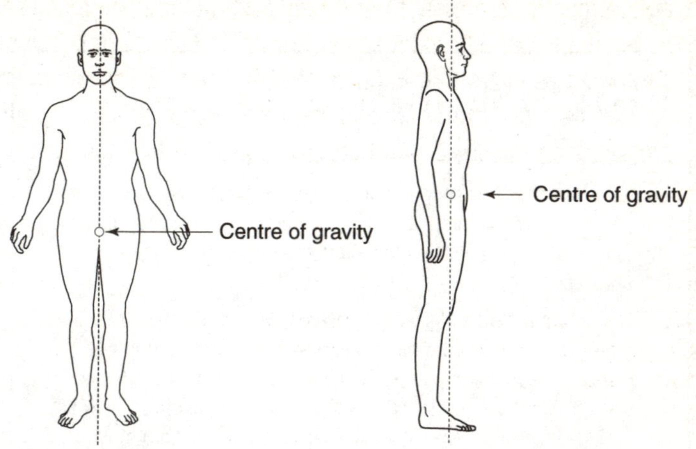

The gravity line drops from the head, through the centre and between the two feet. In the right figure the line drops from the top of the head through the centre, through the front of the knee and through the middle of the feet. In both cases the body weight is distributed more or less equally to either side of this line.

Centring

Progress now

If possible do this exercise while standing.

1   Make sure that your body weight is reasonably well balanced between your left and right feet if you are standing. If you are sitting, distribute your weight evenly between left and right buttocks and between your two feet.

2   Find your own centre of gravity by placing one hand halfway between your navel and your pubic bone. Place your other hand over the corresponding area of your back. The area between your two hands corresponds to your centre of gravity. Pat this section of your body two or three times with your hands then place your hands back at your sides.

3   Now turn your attention to what is going on around you. Use your eyes to notice three things – familiar or unfamiliar. Do the same with your ears – listen to three sounds.

4   Gently switch between concentrating on your centre of gravity and paying attention to your surroundings, breathing gently through your nose.

5   Say 'Keep centre of gravity'. Imagine that your voice is emanating from this centre. Repeat the same phrase internally in your mind's ear.

Practise this centring exercise regularly. Whenever you feel the need to become more centred, simply placing your hands over your centre and repeating the phrase 'Keep centre of gravity' to yourself will help you to reach a centred state.

Centring will give you an effective way to control your feelings of fear at the prospect of presenting. Muscle mass accounts for 35–45 per cent of the total weight of your body. Every cell in your brain connects directly or indirectly to muscle. Centring creatively influences this mind-body system, allowing you to transform anxiety into excitement.

Robert is head of information technology for an international company. He gives regular presentations. Twice a year he speaks to audiences in excess of five hundred. In the past this made him extremely apprehensive. Centring has changed all of that for him:

I find that not only does the work with centring make me feel calmer, it also helps take my mind away from the negative internal dialogue, 'I hope I don't forget my words. I feel faint. I hope I'm not going to keel over.' And so on. Usually just being aware of my centre is sufficient to calm me and keep me on track. Sometimes I just repeat the phrase 'Keep centre of gravity' internally. I imagine that my voice is actually emanating from my centre and radiating out to the edges of my body and beyond. This submerges the negative inner voices and allows me to focus more on my presentation and the audience.

BALANCE AND GROUNDING

Your feet are structured like tripods consisting of the heel and the inner and outer balancing pads, or balls, of each foot. When you stand in a balanced way your body weight is equally distributed between the left and right feet. Approximately 50 per cent of your total body weight drops through the heels. The remaining 50 per cent is more or less equally distributed between the inner and outer balancing pads. This distribution is not static, of course. There will always be some slight oscillation and adjustment in even the most quietly balanced standing.

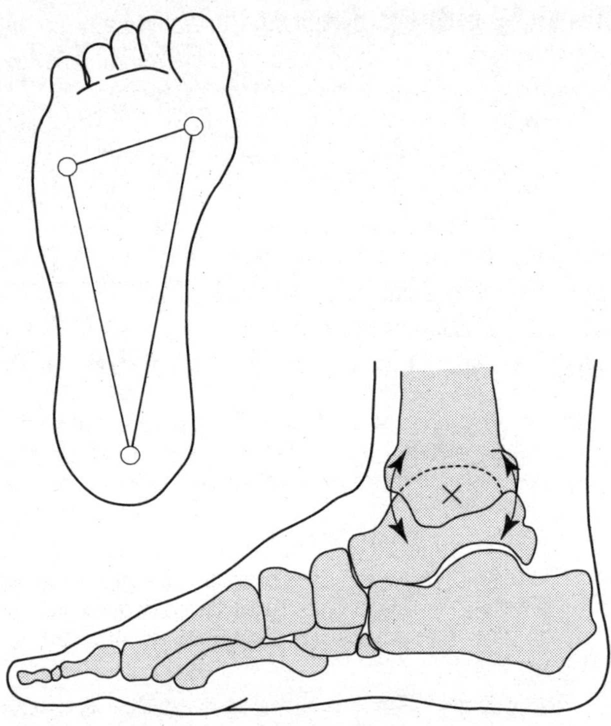

Have you ever noticed people who are physically off balance when they are presenting? Leaning their weight habitually on one leg? Leaning too far forwards or backwards? Legs too far apart, too close together or crossed? More importantly, keep an eye out for the presenters who naturally seem to have a balanced quality. They will almost certainly have a more confident and easy presence.

Progress now

Footprints in the sand

1   Imagine that you are standing with bare feet on some slightly damp sand. Imagine the shape of your footprint in the sand – the roundness of the heels, the outside edge of each foot as it runs up to the little toe, the balls of the feet and the toes. There is virtually no indentation from the inside of the foot where the arch is.

2   You are going to leave two perfect footprints in the sand by ensuring that your body weight is well distributed. Do this by gently swaying your weight from left to right and then from front to back with subtle movements.

3   As you continue making these left/right and front/back adjustments allow your knees to be soft and responsive to the movements.

4   Now focus your attention on your centre, then on the world around you.

5   Gently shuffle your attention between your footprints, your centre and the world around you. Build up a sense of the unity of these interconnected parts.

What upsets your balance?

Have you ever noticed that the sole of one shoe wears out more quickly than the other or that the heels wear quicker than the toes? This could be a result of **habitual weight distribution**, for example leaning on a particular leg when standing. You may also notice this favouritism if you cross your legs when sitting.

And why is it that a bag, even a light one, hangs so well off one shoulder but so badly off the other? This could be because that particular shoulder hitches up habitually to provide a nice hook shape. You might be paying a price, in **muscular tension**, for your handy hook. The heavier the bag is, the more your whole body will compensate by either leaning toward the bag or away from it. This compensation continues to a lesser degree after you put the bag down.

Analyse your weight distribution and day-to-day movements and try to remedy anything that throws you off balance. If you carry a bag, put it down whenever you can — let the train, for example, take its weight rather than your shoulder.

Stop, analyse and correct your movements and posture for a few minutes, here and there, throughout each day. This will help you to become more grounded and centred and will allow your muscles to relax.

John, who suffered from extreme nerves at the start of every presentation, actually positively enjoyed giving presentations after those first few awful minutes were over. He knew his job inside out, he produced relaxed, well-written material and was naturally sociable. His audiences always enjoyed his presentations. The first few minutes were the only grit in the machine for him. What would it be like if he could transform that?

If I could manage the first few minutes more easily I would do more presentations. Doing more presentations would make me a lot more visible within the company. I think I could realistically be up for a senior management position within a few years. I would really like to become a keynote speaker within business circles.

As John started to work on his centring techniques, he found that getting his weight well distributed over his feet was an immensely useful resource. The anxiety evaporated but would come back again very quickly if he leant with too much weight on his left foot. This was almost certainly connected to a desire to rapidly 'exit stage left'. John put a large paperclip in his left shoe. It was very uncomfortable only if he leant on it. When he stood with his weight distributed it was noticeable, but only barely so. As his body began to adapt, John's confidence increased and he is now presenting better than ever.

PERIPHERAL VISION AND PERSONAL SPACE

Stress, the fight/flight response, is notorious for affecting the way in which we use the eyes. The pupils dilate, heightening visual acuity and leading, in many cases, to a tunnelling of the vision. Coupled with tension in the neck and shoulders this can lead to the presenter locking on to certain members of the audience, perceived friends or foes, and consequently leaving the rest of the audience feeling somewhat neglected. Taking responsibility for how you use your eyes not only has a calming influence but it also positively influences the way in which the audience sees you.

More confident, experienced presenters have an ability to encompass the whole audience with one broad, spacious sweep of their eyes. They can also make soft and personal eye contact with individual members of the audience. The first quality, the **broad visual sweep**, helps to bring the presenter to his or her full stature and enhances the impression of a larger than life presence. The second quality lends the presenter a feeling of **approachability** with all its associated qualities.

Peripheral vision

1   Start by remembering your centre and your footprints. Allow your arms to rest at your sides.

2   Link the fingertips of your left and right hands in front of your centre — thumb to thumb, index to index. Smoothly raise your linked fingers until they come to rest, at arm's length, in front of your face.

3   Continue looking straight ahead and move your hands out to your sides until they just disappear from the edges of your vision. Move your hands in and out of the edges of your vision a few times.

4   Bring your hands to rest so that they are just inside your field of peripheral vision. Your arms will be almost fully extended, as if you were preparing to give someone a big hug. Be aware of the big hemisphere of your vision in front, to the left and right, above and below.

5   Keep your sense of this hemisphere of vision as you gently bring your arms down to rest at your sides. Be aware of just how much you can see in your peripheral vision.

Peripheral vision seems to be much more closely connected to our sense of movement and orientation in space than does focused vision in isolation.

Progress now

Walking with an expanded visual field

Look at an object at the other end of the room. Walk towards this object and allow your peripheral vision to remain open. As you walk you may feel as if the walls, floor and ceiling are moving behind you at an equal speed to your movement.

You can expand your visual field at other times – while walking along a road, a corridor, a beach or a country path, for example.

Performing artists of all kinds often seem to have a larger than life presence when they are on stage. Expanding your visual field in this way can help you expand your sense of **personal space**, which is an important stepping stone towards developing your presence.

Personal space

With your arms extended out to your sides, turn in a circle and get a sense of fully occupying the space that you are in. Imagine that you are occupying a sphere of personal space – all around you in a circle, below you and above you. You can brush the boundaries of this space, no matter how large it may be, with your fingertips. Bring your hands down to your sides and continue being aware of your centre, roots, expanded vision and personal space.

Your centre is like a tiny seed from which your presence extends in all directions. Excellent presenters have the ability to adjust the size of their personal presence, as appropriate, for different contexts and situations.

A good 'home base' for personal space or presence is one that is at arms' length all around you. Practise this with your peripheral vision and arms gently extended in the privacy of your home, in different-sized rooms. Remember to come back to home base, arms' length around you, each time.

PERCEPTUAL POSITIONS AND PERSONAL RELATIONS

Why do some people naturally have a wide range and depth of understanding of all kinds of people, issues and situations? What allows them to penetrate to the heart of a situation and deal with it with flexibility, grace and elegance? When it comes to mentally rehearsing a presentation, or any performance situation, you can do it from at least three different but complementary points of view:

- Your own viewpoint
- The perspective of the audience
- The vantage point of a detached yet kindly observer.

Each individual has their own unique way of viewing the world as well as a contribution to make to any given situation. But with each of these unique viewpoints comes an equally special set of limitations.

At any time each of us is capable of consciously processing approximately seven chunks of information. For example, most people will just about be able to remember a seven-digit phone number. A nine-digit number will be more difficult. If, however, you divide the nine-digit number into three chunks of three digits each you will again find the whole number easier to recall. How much you can recall is also influenced by chunk size, e.g. seven leaves, seven twigs, seven branches, seven trees, seven forests.

In law courts different witnesses give evidence on the same event. Depending on their differing vantage points they may see and hear different things and arrive at quite different conclusions. Each witness has their own unique way of selecting which seven chunks of the situation they will attend to. This multiplicity of information enables the judge, as an observer of the proceedings, to develop a fuller picture of the situation.

Each of us is capable of viewing life events and personal and business relationships from a multiplicity of perspectives. The more perspectives we have, the more chunks of information are available to us to guide our choices and behaviour.

PERCEPTUAL TOOLS

The radio reporter revisited

You may like to use a tape recorder for the perceptual position exercises in the following section. The tape recorder takes the place of a fascinated listener who hangs on to every word of your mental rehearsal strategy as you broadcast it out loud. Your job is to create, like the radio broadcaster, as vivid a mental picture as possible for this listener. It does not matter whether *you* see the pictures or not – even if you are not a natural visualizer you will slowly start to increase your ability through using this method. Just as in real radio programmes you could do the radio report from different points of view.

A little black book

It is useful to carry a small notebook with you as the VMBR strategy also works with writing. It is not only useful for writing mental rehearsal scripts but also for making notes of moments of creative insight and inspiration.

Mental rehearsal ingredients

Mental rehearsal is all very well, but you may be wondering what to rehearse. Here are a few 'openers' — safe, easy chunks of words and language, to get you started.

People who are giving presentations are often, quite rightly, encouraged to pause powerfully before launching into their presentation. Many speakers, especially when they feel anxious, find this difficult to do. When muscles are overly tense a pause of a few seconds can seem like a long time. Your centre of gravity is a useful and creative location in which to place your attention during those critical few seconds.

1   Pause for a few seconds and direct your attention on your centre of gravity before you introduce yourself to an imaginary audience. Recite a piece of poetry, a limerick, a nursery rhyme — anything that amuses you. Pause, and recentre at the end of each line.

2   Now use a more realistic introduction e.g. '*My name is* (your name) *and I work in* (your job title) *and today I am going to speak about* (your choice of subject).'

First perceptual position: your own viewpoint

In this, the first perceptual position, you stand inside your own skin, look out of your own eyes and have your own habitual thoughts and feelings about the world around you and your relationships within it. From here you engage fully and vitally with the world around you. It is the place from which your choices and decisions are ultimately implemented.

However, you can become stuck in habitual grooves of thought, feeling and attitude which reduce your ability to deal with the challenges of daily life. Travelling around the other perceptual positions, then returning to and updating the first position, is a great help for getting back on track.

First position language and mental rehearsal are characterized by the **first-person pronoun**:

'I'm here. I've planned and prepared my words and visual aids. I've centred myself, warmed up my voice and practised my moves. I am now walking on to the stage. I see and hear my audience. I am ready to speak.'

Second perceptual position: the audience's viewpoint

This, the second perceptual position, is as if you occupy someone else's body, habitual thoughts and feelings, look out at the world through their eyes and gain a deeper understanding of their feelings, values, needs and perspectives.

At its most basic level this means **knowing your audience**:

- What do they want to get out of your presentation?
- If you haven't met any of your audience before, try doing a bit of research on the group or company that you are speaking to.
- Knowing just a little of their current concerns really can go a long way.
- Knowing some of the current language or jargon is also helpful if used skilfully and sparingly.

The second perceptual position can be used to identify with a member of the audience and observe yourself from their perspective. Something that does not seem to work well from the presenter's point of view may, in fact, work brilliantly from the audience's perspective – and vice versa. Feedback from trusted friends and colleagues helps with this, as does recording your presentations.

At a deeper level, the second position involves putting yourself in the other person's shoes and, for a short period, taking on their personal viewpoint:

- Imagine yourself sitting observing your presentation from the point of view of an audience member.
- As you go through your presentation, watch and listen to yourself from the perspective of that audience member.
- How does it make you feel? What impact does your presentation have on you, the audience member? Would you do anything differently as a result?

The language of the second position is characterized by the **third-person pronoun**:

'***He/she** is now walking on to the stage. **He/she** is pausing and centring him/herself. **He/she** is looking out to the audience. **He/she** is starting to speak.*'

This language can also be 'warmed up' by speaking from the perspective of a friendly audience member:

'Celia is now walking on to the stage. And now she is pausing. Celia is starting to speak.'

Once you have done this, come back to the first position:

- Now that you have seen your presentation from the point of view of a friendly audience, how would you do things differently?

- Given the audience's background and their reasons for listening to you, what parts of the jigsaw could you fill in to complete the picture of your presentation?

Third perceptual position: a detached vantage point

In this, the third perceptual position, you become a detached, wise observer of yourself and your way of relating to others. Your focus of vision is broad. The third position utilizes distance to decrease the emotional enmeshment that many experience in difficult situations and enables you to see where the patterns of your own feelings, values and needs and those of others dovetail. It also helps you to perceive where you and they are not meeting — and how to adjust your behaviour accordingly.

The language of the third position is that of the **descriptive observer**:

'He/she is walking slowly onto the stage. He/she is pausing and centring. He/she is looking out confidently to the audience. He/she is now speaking clearly.'

Third position can be made warmer and more connected by using the performer's name:

'Celia is walking slowly onto the stage now. Celia is pausing and centring herself. Celia is now starting to speak clearly.'

With practise this warm sense of connection can become the voice of the personal coach who is calling out encouragement from the sidelines whenever it is needed.

Third position has wide enough vision to track the relationship between audience and presenter:

'The audience are talking amongst themselves. Celia is walking out onto stage. She pauses and the audience becomes aware of her presence. Celia starts to speak.'

In *Why I Write*, **George Orwell** describes a form of inner writing that is uncannily close to the third perceptual position:

... for fifteen years or more, I was carrying out a literary exercise of a quite different kind: this was the making up of a continuous 'story' about myself, a sort of diary existing only in the mind. I believe this is a common habit of children and adolescents. As a very small child I used to imagine that I was, say, Robin Hood, and picture myself as the hero of thrilling adventures, but quite soon my 'story' ceased to be narcissistic in a crude way and became more and more a mere description of what I was doing and the things I saw. For minutes at a time this kind of thing would be running through my head: 'He pushed the door open and entered the room. A yellow beam of sunlight, filtering through the muslin curtains, slanted on to the table, where a match-box, half-open, lay beside the inkpot. With his right hand in his pocket he moved across to the window. Down in the street a tortoiseshell cat was chasing a dead leaf,' etc.

etc. This habit continued until I was about twenty-five, right through my non-literary years. Although I had to search, and did search, for the right words, I seemed to be making this descriptive effort almost against my will, under a kind of compulsion from outside. The 'story' must, I suppose, have reflected the styles of the various writers I admired at different ages, but so far as I remember it always had the same meticulous descriptive quality.

DEALING WITH DIFFICULTIES

People find perceptual shifts harder to achieve with individuals whom they consider to be difficult or an adversary. Understanding the other person's point of view, it must be emphasized, does not necessarily mean agreeing with them. It does, however, make it easier to empathize with them.

In a 1950s experiment on anger, the unwitting volunteers were insulted by one of the experimenters who then quickly left the room. Unaware that they had been set up, the volunteers became angry. Another experimenter explained that the person who had left the room was having a particularly difficult time in their personal life at the moment. The volunteers calmed down very quickly on hearing this information.

In the above example the volunteers shifted from first position (self), to second position and then into the calmness of third position before returning, calmed down and more compassionate, to first position. This kind of quick shuffle certainly makes it easier to deal with people or situations that you might normally consider to be difficult.

There is a native American expression that says you should not judge another person until you have walked a month in their moccasins. In other words, no matter how crazy their behaviour might seem from your point of view, it will have an internal logic or coherence from where they are standing:

There is a positive intention behind every communication.

Is the above statement true? Not in any absolute sense. Is it useful? Incredibly. Before you go on to your next task of the day, try centring yourself and think about some of the people with whom you will be having minor meetings or interactions. Repeat the above phrase to yourself a few times. This centring will reduce your anxiety and increase your flexibility by taking you quickly and automatically through the three perceptual positions. It will increase your respect for other people's point of view, decrease friction and open the door to the possibility of harmony or at least respectful disagreement.

PAUL MARWAHA

Paul Marwaha is an award-winning film and television cameraman. I was fortunate enough to work with him on several presentation courses. Paul's official role was to film the delegates as they gave their presentations. The trainers and delegates would then review the film for the purposes of feedback. In between presentations we would do various warm-up and preparation exercises. When not filming, Paul would occasionally join in the exercises but mostly he would sit quietly in the background taking in the general dynamic of what was happening in the room. Paul had been sitting in the background observing courses for a lot longer than I had been standing in the foreground running courses. He had seen a lot more trainers in action, with their different styles and approaches, than I ever had. What a fantastic resource! Any time I was feeling a little bit stuck and not quite sure what direction to head in I would simply have a quick word with Paul. From his third position perspective he would accurately assess the atmosphere of the group and suggest a good exercise, the right words to say or simply recommend that great tradition – the tea break. Sometimes when my co-trainer was leading a group activity I would just go and sit beside Paul and soak up the group dynamic from this third position vantage point. This became an anchor for me even when Paul was not around. Just sitting at the edge of the room noticing the patterns often gave me an idea of where to go next.

Keep on people watching like Paul – it is a wonderful presenter's tool.

STATE YOUR GOALS IN POSITIVE TERMS

- Do you want to be able to speak with greater calmness and composure?

- Perhaps you would like to speak with more conviction and passion?

- Would you like to know how to construct a presentation more easily?

- Or maybe you are constantly involved in a process of continually developing your skills?

Whatever your goals, it is immensely helpful to state them in terms that are positive. It is easier to visualize what you *do* want than what you do not want. Consequently 'I want to be calmer and more composed' is preferable to 'I do not want to be frightened'; and 'I want to be able to express my thoughts in a clear and systematic way' is preferable to 'I don't want my words to come out in a jumble.'

Of course, it is also very important to formulate goals for your audience e.g. 'I want the audience to be so stimulated by my presentation that they think about it all the way home.' This could lead to some more specific goals e.g. 'I want the audience to be so stimulated by my presentation that they buy my product/service.'

Progress now

Sometimes people can find it very difficult to formulate a positive outcome, usually because they have been immersed in a limiting mind-set which has reduced their horizons. A simple tip for dealing with this is to describe your goal first in negative language – 'I don't want to be terrified while presenting' – then to describe it again in the exact opposite way – 'I want to be deliriously happy while presenting'. You can then start to fine tune: 'I want to be confident . . .'; 'I want to be in tune with the audience'; 'I want to enjoy being in tune with my audience.' Keep adjusting until your stated goal makes you feel positive and relaxed.

CHAPTER 4

How Committed Are You?

> It is not enough to have knowledge; one must also apply it. It is not enough to have wishes; one must also accomplish.
>
> JOHANN WOLFGANG VON GOETHE

> Until one is committed there is hesitancy, the chance to draw back, always ineffectiveness. Whatever you can do, or believe you can, begin it. Boldness has genius, power and magic in it.
>
> W.N. MURRAY, THE SCOTTISH HIMALAYAN EXPEDITION, 1951

GO FOR IT

Whatever your current level of skills, identify an opportunity for presenting — an opportunity which will require you to crank up your skills by a few notches. Not something that will make you panic but something that will stretch you a bit. Then put yourself on the spot. Set the date. Advertise the fact. Let it be known publicly.

There is nothing like potential embarrassment for mobilizing one's resources. Once you have set the date and advertised the fact, get your team to work on preparing you for the big event. Think of giving a presentation as a team sport, rather than a solo sport. You don't have a team? Behind every great woman or man, and their presentations, there are family, friends or colleagues.

Now practise the skills that will ensure that you do yourself justice. You have to do your training as part of the team.

Planning – step one

1 Practise your centring regularly

There are more suggestions about how to approach this later in this chapter and in the following chapter.

2 Choose the subject for your presentation

You may already know what this is. For novel and fresh ways of presenting your subject, see Chapter 6.

3 Estimate how long it will take you to get ready to present this subject in public

How much time will you need for research, structuring, solo rehearsal, rehearsal with your team and finally public presentation? If you are the type of person who tends to be late for things, double your most optimistic estimate.

4 Open up your diary and find or create the necessary preparation and rehearsal time

Planning – step two

1   **Do your research using all the means available to you**

2   **Start to structure and organize your material**

Chapter 6 is full of suggestions about how to do this.

Planning – step three

Your **message** – the words of your presentation – is of paramount importance, but the **non-verbal** component is also vital. To make sure that your words are seeds sown in fertile ground you need to give sufficient time and attention to the non-verbal elements.

Allow sufficient time to plan the words and the non-verbal elements. Revise your original estimate of the time needed.

Centre and rehearse

1   **Call your muse on the move**
    Do this in your 'in-between' moments, such as waiting in queues. Let your mind wander to your presentation.

2   **Solo rehearse chunks of your presentation**
    Practise three opening lines of your presentation. Practise three lines from the middle. And practise three closing lines. The emphasis here is on physical, spatial and vocal presence.

3   **Do a solo run through of your whole presentation**

4   **Rehearse the presentation with your team**
    The team could be colleagues, family members or even dolls.

5   **Do it for real!**

Planning – step four

Get as much constructive feedback as possible before and after.

Expect to continue learning and improving consciously and deliberately and unconsciously and spontaneously.

Most of us need to put in a bit of practice to get progressively nearer to that enviable state of connection between self, subject and audience. **Commitment** is the vital link that will take you from that demotivating feeling of 'have to' present to the highly motivated place of 'wanting to' present.

So what factors **reduce** motivation and commitment?

1   Fear about presenting or some aspect of presenting.

2   The perceived size of the task.

3   Lack of self-belief.

4   'Square peg in a round' hole syndrome – a poor fit between person and job.

To a greater or lesser degree, all of these commitment-reducing factors will influence and reinforce each other. The good news is that a change in any one of these areas will encourage change in all of the others. The next few sections will show how to effect these changes.

Now be a bit more positive and consider what the commitment-**increasing** factors might be:

1   Developing increasing confidence about presenting or about aspects of presenting.

2   Cutting the task down into easy, bite-sized chunks.

3   Deliberately cultivating self-belief.

4   Developing a good fit between self and job.

REDUCING FEAR AND INCREASING CONFIDENCE

In situations of real or imagined threat, a group of responses called the 'fight or flight' syndrome come into force. This syndrome acts by releasing hormones, including adrenaline, into the bloodstream. These hormones make the muscles more tense and speed up both breathing and heart rate. The muscles that connect shoulders, neck and head are often the first to contract in the 'startle' or fight/flight pattern, causing the head to be pulled back and down towards the body's centre of gravity. Blood flow is diverted from the surface and the core of the body to the muscles, with a consequent raising of blood pressure. In this situation a person's face will often drain of colour as the blood moves away from the skin surface.

Fortunately there are many ways of reducing and creatively channelling the energy of the fight/flight pattern to enhance your performance and communication skills. You will already be familiar with some of them from the previous chapter. We shall look at some additional, related strategies in this chapter. We shall also look at how these quick and effective personal resource boosters can massively enhance the use of your voice and body during presentations.

If you are one of the lucky few who does not experience nerves, do to try these techniques anyway — they are foundation techniques for using your voice and body to maximum effect.

How to keep your head

The critical moment of starting to speak brings into play many inappropriate habits associated with the fight/flight reflex. The most common vocal habits are associated with sucking in a large breath before speaking. This causes a dramatic increase in the contraction of muscle groups that have nothing directly to do with breathing — the neck and throat muscles, shoulders, upper arms, upper chest and back — which leads to a visible displacement of head balance at the moment of breathing in. A more general awareness of balancing the head easily and efficiently on top of your spine in the non-demanding moments of day-to-day life will help you to keep your head during the more pressurized times. Because the head is so close to the voice box and the mouth, a better balance of your head and alignment of your spine will also positively affect the way that you speak.

The skull

Trace around the base of your skull until your fingers come to the soft, hollowish area just behind your jaw joint. Point your fingers, through your neck, towards each other. About 2.5 cm before your fingers would meet if they could is the approximate location of the **atlanto-occipital** joint, the place where the top of your spine joins the base of your skull (see next page).

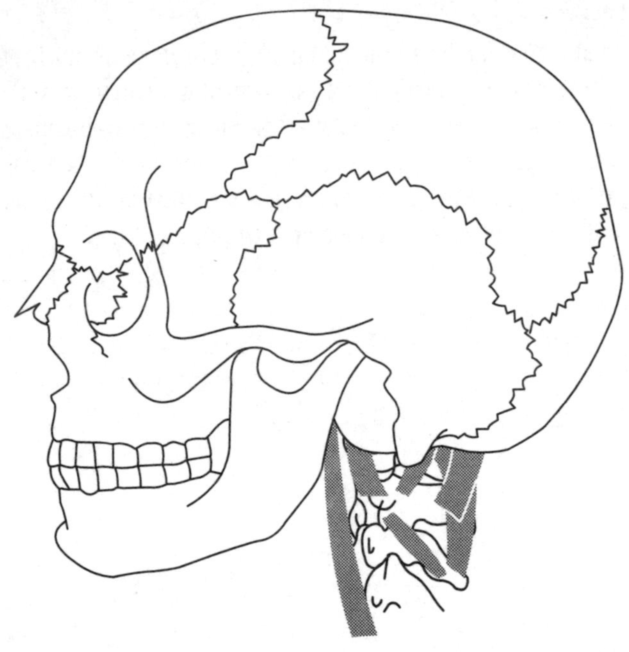

The atlanto-occipital joint and sub-occipital muscles.

The spine

The spine is longer and substantially thicker than most people realize. Its weight-bearing parts are located deep in the core of the torso. Understanding this fact significantly contributes to an enhanced sense of inner support. The lumbar section of the spine occupies at least a quarter of the depth of the body. The spine occupies at least a quarter of the depth of the ribcage and up to half the depth of the neck. By the time you add spinal muscles to the picture the spine looks even more substantial. The spine is like a supremely well-jointed and muscular 'fifth limb' that stretches up from the tailbone to support and balance the globe of the head within space.

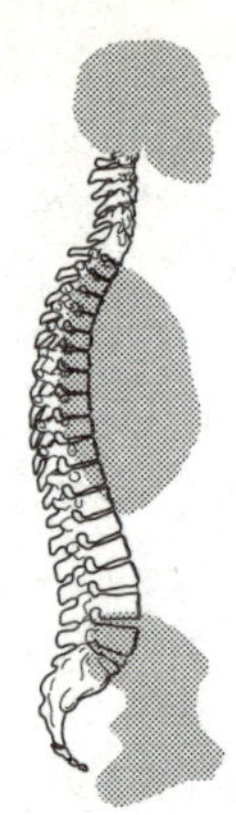

The spine.

To put this in a practical context, think of a puppet string attached to the top of your head which initiates the release of the neck muscles and the easy balancing of the head on top of a lengthening spine. If the puppet string is placed too far forward, your head tips back; too far back and it drops forwards. If the puppet string is placed directly above the area where the spine joins the skull, the head will tend to come into an easy, level balance on top of the spine which will encourage the spine to lengthen.

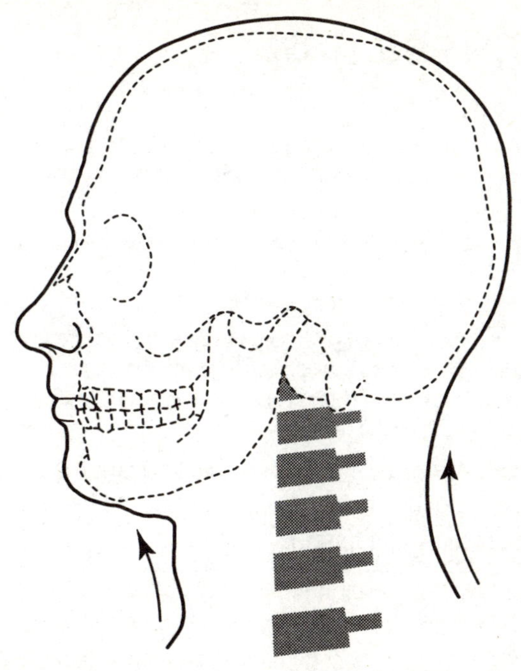

The puppet string.

Progress now

Your puppet string

1   With both hands, trace up from your atlanto-occipital areas directly past the earholes until your fingers meet at the top of your head.

2   Tap gently on this spot for a minute. Now bring your hands down to rest at your sides. You will probably still feel the sensation of the tapping for a few moments. This area, directly above the top of your spine, is where your imaginary puppet string attaches.

3   With the help of the imaginary puppet string, guide yourself into a state that is more balanced around your line of gravity (see page 45). Do not make any muscular effort to change the way you are standing — let the puppet string do it for you.

It is useful to do this exercise with the help of a friend or a mirror as you might try at first to tilt your head forwards or to the side to meet your hand.

Emotion, breathing and your voice

In the early 1940s, the surgeon **William Faulkner** carried out an experiment in which he measured his patients' physical responses to stressful then to pleasant thoughts. When his patients thought of something unpleasant, he noticed that the movement of their diaphragm became restricted, shallow and irregular. These breathing changes were accompanied by a corresponding tightening of the throat and negative changes in the characteristic quality of the patient's speaking voice. When, on the other hand, his patients thought of something pleasant, the movement of their diaphragm became expansive and regular and the levels of tension in the throat were reduced. All of this was accompanied by positive changes in the characteristics of their voices.

In the following exercise you can compare the effects that stressful and pleasant thoughts have on you and your voice. You will be recalling and reliving an example of each emotional state in turn. So please do make sure that the unpleasant one is quite mild. The pleasant one can be very pleasant indeed!

Exercise 1: Observing restriction

1   Think of a time when you felt mildly pressured and restricted. Remember this using your mind's eyes, ears and feelings – what you saw around you, what you heard and also what you felt. Stay fully in this state for a couple of minutes.

2   Now look around the room. Does it look any less bright or any less friendly than before? Do you feel taller or shorter? Do you feel wider or narrower? What size does your personal space seem to be (indicate this with your hands)?

3   Walk around the room. Is your walking lighter or heavier?

4   Vocalize an 'aahh' sound. How easy or difficult is it to vocalize?

5   Now introduce yourself to an imaginary audience:

'Hello. My name is __________ *and today I am going to speak to you about* __________*.'*

Exercise 2: Observing and cultivating ease

1   Move and stretch to dissipate the effects of the last exercise.

2   Remember a time when you felt on top of the world. Recall and relive this experience – what you were seeing, hearing and feeling. Stay fully in this state for a couple of minutes and allow yourself to release your breath outwards for a little bit longer, slightly more slowly than you normally would. Can you allow your breath back in at an easy, unforced flowing pace? Let this top of the world feeling spread, little by little, across your whole body.

3   Look around the room again. Is it any brighter or friendlier now? Do you feel shorter or taller? Narrower or wider? How large is your personal space now?

4   Take a walk around the room. Is your walking heavier or lighter?

5   Vocalize an 'aahh' sound. Notice how your voice feels and sounds different from the first exercise.

6   Introduce yourself again to your imaginary audience.

You have just taken the first step in freeing your body and liberating your voice!

Ultimately it will become clear that your body, feelings and mind are part of one system. A change in any one of them – body, feelings or mind – will affect all the others.

THE SIZE OF THE PERCEIVED TASK

The larger a task is, the more it has to be broken down into easily attainable sub-tasks or chunks. Working on small chunks helps to bring the presenter/performer into the here-and-now and therefore more into their body, which is the foundation stone of the voice. Unlike daily life, where one activity slides into another, a presentation has a more clearly defined beginning, middle and end. This makes it easier to practise small, specific and manageable chunks at a time.

Your emotional state

When you have a presentation coming up, you may feel that you have simply got too much on your plate. This is usually linked to your personal state – physical, emotional and mental. When you are feeling low, the size of a task can expand dramatically in your mind and make you feel even more physically weighed down. On the other hand, when you feel awake and refreshed, tasks can seem a great deal smaller.

> At 40 I am beginning to learn the mechanism of my own brain. How to get the greatest amount of pleasure and work out of it. The secret is, I think, always so to contrive that work is pleasant.
>
> Virginia Woolf

Just how do you contrive that your work is always pleasant?

Hasten slowly and pleasantly

Progress now

1   Make a list of six things that you have to do:

____

____

____

____

____

2   Now make yourself very tense and imagine yourself doing the activities. How motivating is this? How committed do you feel? Tension often leads to fatigue and slump. Get yourself into a heavy, slumped state and imagine yourself doing the activities on your list.

3   Now take a minute or two to centre yourself and open up your sense of personal space. Think through item one on your list. Pause and refresh your centring for a few seconds. Now think through item two. Pause and re-centre. Repeat until you reach the end of your list and centre yourself once again. You will be much more likely to see your list of activities through to their conclusion when you approach them in this way.

Later in the chapter you will work on some bite-sized chunks of a whole presentation i.e. the opening and closing remarks. You will practise them in a physically, spatially and vocally centred way. You will then identify some real-life situations in which to practise them so that they are available to you, ready and waiting, during more demanding presentations.

Chunking

Many aspects of centring help you to cut tasks down to size. Many of your centring exercises can be practised in the middle of boring day-to-day activities, such as waiting in a queue or at traffic lights. This will enable you to mentally rehearse chunks of your presentation. Not only will this cut down the frustration that is often felt at these moments, it will also positively affect your performance in the moments that follow.

A client who had been having some difficulty in establishing rapport with his customers found that by practising these skills with the people who worked on their reception desks, he could improve his relationship with his customers:

It was just a two or three minute walk from the station to my client's office. I walked slowly, remembering my centre, my width and my height. I was actually enjoying the hustle and bustle of central London all around me. I walked up to reception and waited while the receptionist finished a call. I smiled at her and told her my name and whom I had come to visit. Her face lit up and I was surprised when she said, 'Oh, what a lovely clear voice you have! You've got no idea how many people mumble and rush when they come to reception!'

I was slightly embarrassed, but mostly pleasantly surprised by this response. I wasn't even really thinking about my voice, but somehow the centring had worked its magic. The feeling continued in the lift and into my customer's office. The meeting with my customer was much more comfortable and constructive and I am glad to say it has continued that way.

I've now turned this into part of my strategy. Reception can be an unrewarding job — if I make their day a little brighter the next time I arrive I'll usually get a genuine smile and greeting from them, which sets me up for the business I am about to do.

Give some thought to the 'in-between' moments of your life — the places where, instead of becoming frustrated, you can practise your centring skills. Think also of low-risk places where you can practise making calm and composed entrances followed by clear and centred introductions, greetings or opening lines. Do this regularly in low-risk settings and you will find it becomes increasingly available to you in your more stretching situations.

SELF-BELIEF

In 1968 **Rosenthal & Jacobson** carried out an experiment designed to assess how the expectation of teachers would affect the performance of their pupils.

The children in the experimental group were a random mix of ability levels – above average, average and below average – and were sorted into their respective primary grade levels. The children in the control group classes were sorted similarly for ability and age. The only difference was that the teachers of the experimental group classes were told to expect surprising gains in intellectual ability over the rest of the school year. At the end of the year, when they were all tested, the children in the experimental 'high expectation' group showed significantly greater intellectual gains than the children in the control group.

> Overall, the children from whom the teachers had been led to expect greater intellectual gain showed a significantly greater gain than did the children of the control group, thereby supporting the 'Pygmalion' hypothesis.

Rosenthal & Jacobson 1968

Although people often talk about the 'weight' of other people's expectations, they can also work in the opposite direction – the right kind of expectation can actually buoy the recipient up and help to set them on course. If you are fortunate you will have received this kind of support at some point in your life. There will be times, however, when you will have to do this for yourself. The next few pages will show you how.

Internal voices – talking your walk

A group is carrying out a simple exercise to be done in pairs. One of the partners – the 'goal achiever' – chooses a simple task to carry out, such as walking across the room to pick up an object and then putting it down somewhere else. The other partner – the 'nag' – gives the moving partner the benefit of some critical instructions but in a nagging tone of voice, too fast for the person to assimilate. The instructions are couched entirely in negative language:

Don't be off-centre! Don't be ungrounded! Don't tunnel your vision! Don't stiffen your neck! Don't pull your head down! Don't shorten and narrow your back! Don't tighten your jaw, legs, arms! Don't hold your breath! Don't be slow!

Imagine that you are either receiving or giving these instructions. How do they affect you physically, emotionally and mentally? You probably won't be surprised to hear that the goal achievers looked completely off-centre, ungrounded and stiff as they moved. Once they had completed their task they were tested for balance by the nag. Unsurprisingly they were quite unstable and wobbly. What is surprising is that when the goal achievers applied a balance test to the nags, the nags were also very wobbly and off-centre.

In the discussion afterwards the achievers said that the instructions sounded and felt like this: *'OffcentreUngrounded TunnelyourvisionStiffenyourneckPullyourheaddownHoldyourbreath Beslow!'*

How did it make them feel?

AAAAGH!' and ***'GGRRRRR!'***

And how motivated did it make them feel?

'FORGET IT!'

None of the nags took pleasure in their role. In fact, most of them said that they found the exercise had as negative an effect on themselves as it had on the goal achiever.

The nags have now transformed into 'coaches' and are giving encouraging directions in a pleasant tone and with appropriate pacing:

> Take a moment to remember your centre . . . Good . . . and as you remember your centre so you can also get more grounded . . . and allow your visual field to open and expand . . . And when you are good and ready you can walk across the room and move your object . . . Move at a pace that is comfortable to you . . . Your back is long and wide . . . head balancing easily on top of your spine . . . Excellent . . . Breathe smoothly and flowingly as you walk . . .

On completing their task they again test each other for balance. This time they are quite stable, flexible and confident. Both coach and goal achiever are full of calm energy and ready for the next task on the agenda, whatever it may be.

What was the most significant part of the exercise? Apparently the most valuable experience was that of being the coach . . . after all, if you could be that nurturing, encouraging and motivating for someone else, why not be just as loving to yourself?

Progress now

The next time you have to give someone instructions, such as directions, try doing it with a warm, encouraging tone and with appropriate pacing. Keep your eyes and ears alive so that you can see and hear how they are responding. This will automatically affect the rate at which you speak and pause.

PERSON AND JOB — GETTING THE FIT RIGHT

The general theme of this chapter has been about going from the feeling of 'having to present' to 'wanting to present'. This will be much easier if you are already doing a job that you want to do rather than feel you have to do. It is even more important to be able to get into a state where you want to present despite being in a job that you are not entirely happy with. At the very least you can cultivate the 'want to' feeling in your presentation style, even if you are not entirely charmed with the presentation content. Use your presentations as an opportunity to prime yourself so that you are ready to take on your dream job when the occasion arises.

Phyllis had spent many years working as a librarian for a particular employer. In the beginning it was the right job, in the right place, with the right people. Unfortunately, her conditions of employment deteriorated progressively over a number of years until it became the wrong job, in the wrong place, at the wrong time and full of very unhappy people. It had become so intolerable that Phyllis was strongly considering leaving the job without having alternative employment in place. Jobs for librarians were few and far between and, because she did not have a degree, Phyllis was not hopeful about her prospects at interview. This had the effect of diminishing her performance at the actual interview, so Phyllis decided to take a two-day presentation course.

When people work under the unhappy conditions described above, their self-esteem can often take a bit of a knock. During the first part of the course Phyllis was overly critical of her efforts during her presentations. She received firm encouragement from the trainer, who would brook no contradiction. Phyllis began to give herself the benefit of the doubt. She started enjoying herself more and her performance improved.

Shortly afterwards, Phyllis went for an interview at a high profile academic institution in Glasgow:

> I thought 'OK, Phyllis, this is your big chance so let's make the most of it. I'm determined that I am going to enjoy this interview. Centre yourself . . . Allow your spine to lengthen . . . Breathe out gently and smoothly . . . I'm going to extend a very positive, calm feeling to the interviewers . . . In fact I'm going to interview them . . . I'm going to ask them some questions.'
>
> And I did feel calm. I did feel friendly. I did ask questions. And, even if I say so myself, I did a brilliant interview. I got the job and it's lovely. I found out later that I was the only librarian without a degree to get a job in this institution.

Not only did Phyllis get herself the ideal job but, once she had grasped the core principles for making presentations, she gathered increasing momentum and there was no stopping her.

CHAPTER 5

Better Than What?

Attempt easy tasks as if they were difficult, and difficult tasks as if they were easy, in the one case that confidence may not fall asleep, in the other that it may not be dismayed.

BALTASAR GRACIAN

USING YOUR SKILLS

We all know people who are great speakers over a cup of coffee or on the phone, at home or informally in the office — fluent, earnest, fresh-thinking, witty and passionate. Yet put that person in front of an audience, and their verbal facility disappears.

This, in its own way, is an automatic response. Although the adrenaline-fuelled reaction is remarkably similar from person to person, the circumstances that stimulate it vary tremendously. For some people it is not the size of audience but their status that is important. Presenting to a peer group will terrify some, while presenting to those with greater authority or influence scares others. Size is a significant factor for many but there is not much agreement on what constitutes a large audience — ten, twenty, two hundred? For others small audiences trigger fear. Some people feel more comfortable presenting than they do with ordinary social interaction.

We are all intensely individual and deeply unique but we are all wrought from the same basic ingredients — body, voice, language and awareness of other people. Even quite minor adjustments to the proportions of these ingredients can lead to huge changes in the way that we feel, express ourselves and engage with others, without compromising our individuality.

How can you create a response to presentation nerves that will allow you to have the same quality of rapport with an audience as you have during your best moments such as informal conversation?

In this chapter, you will work on the non-verbal, physical, spatial and vocal elements of rapport-building, including:

- Using your eyes and ears to observe the body language and voice of other individuals
- Adjusting your body language and voice to gain rapport with other individuals
- Transferring individual rapport skills into audience contexts
- Eye contact
- Noticing potential friends and allies in the audience
- Taking ownership of your space
- Adjusting your personal space according to the size and type of your audience
- Strengthening your competence and confidence with challenging people and situations
- Using feedback effectively.

HUMAN MIRRORS

Rapport can be developed **physically** by mirroring a person's body language – arms, legs, posture, shoulders and face. It can be developed **vocally** by reflecting the pitch, rhythm, volume and tempo of someone's voice. Physical and vocal **mirroring** can help put the person you are speaking to at ease. It also develops your sensory acuity – you will see and hear the other person much more accurately and clearly. If you work on these rapport skills with a trusted partner, you can then transfer them into group-based presentations of any size.

Progress now

Mirroring

Work with a trusted partner for this exercise.

1   Copy precisely the posture, hand and arm gestures, foot and leg positions, head, neck and shoulder carriage and facial expressions of your partner as they speak.

2   Now copy your partner's gestures in a more subtler manner. For example, large arm movements could be mirrored with much smaller but similar hand movements. This minimalist mirroring allows you to remain centred and aligned with yourself and yet build a bridge to your partner at the same time.

3   Do the opposite of your partner — for example, when he or she leans left, you should lean right.

Mirroring in daily life

Mirroring is a natural process. It is one reason why family members or close friends tend to stand, walk and talk in similar ways.

A note of caution does have to be sounded here, however. We all know individuals who drain our energy or jangle our nerves despite being the loveliest of people. Because they are approachable and nice it is easy to get hooked into their prevailing destructive emotional state, which can drag you in a negative direction.

This also works the other way with positive people with high levels of energy. We hook into and get drawn up towards their higher energy level and emotional state and walk away from them feeling refreshed and happier. This is the kind of strategy you need to adopt for presenting to groups — hook your audience verbally and non-verbally and start to gently open up the appropriate energy and mood for the occasion.

Vocal mirroring

Remember some of the vocal characteristics from Chapter 2:

- Volume
- Pace and rhythm
- Articulation
- Pitch and variation
- Resonance
- Silence and pause

Think of the origin of each of these types of voice: do they seem to come from the throat, the chest or the head? How would you need to hold your body to make that sound yourself? Once you have begun to develop an ear for the variations in the ways that other people speak, you will find it easier to mirror different vocal styles.

EYE CONTACT

As with many other aspects of presenting, there are no hard and fast rules concerning eye contact. There was a time, not so long ago, when popular advice to presenters or interviewees was 'Make sure you give good eye contact'. All too often this could turn into an uncomfortable battle of wills with the first person to break eye contact feeling like the loser.

It is quite normal to make and break eye contact. If you watch any conversation between two people who are reasonably comfortable with one another you will see this happen in its own, almost dance-like rhythm. Most people find it disconcerting if eye contact is not held for long enough or is held for too long. The state of mind of the person giving or receiving the eye contact also influences the comfort factor positively or negatively.

As a general rule, the more centred you are the more pleasant or acceptable your quality of eye contact will be. The guidelines for new instructors of the martial art Aikido state that a teacher should have 'soft and friendly eyes'. This advice holds good for most presentation circumstances, as it tends to increase your authority rather than diminish it. If your eye contact is hard, your listeners are likely to become less receptive. If your eye contact is soft yet direct, your listeners will soften and your information will be absorbed more readily by their brains and memory.

Progress now

Imagine that there is a triangle on the face of the person you are looking at or speaking to. The base of the triangle spreads from the bridge of the nose to the edges of the eyebrows. The sides sweep down both sides of the face, past the corners of the mouth, to meet at the point of the chin.

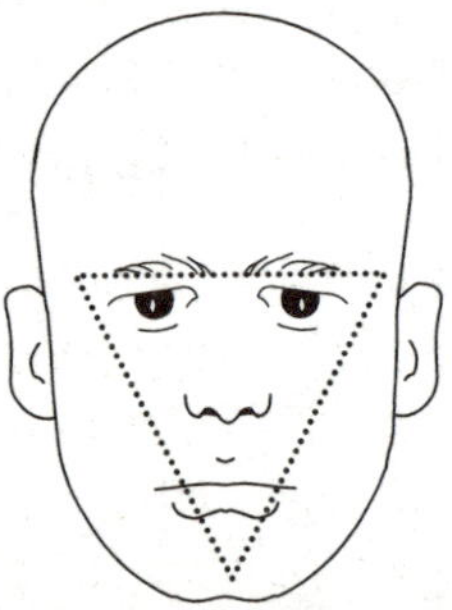

If you look anywhere within this triangle, the recipient will still feel as if you are looking into their eyes.

How long should eye contact last?

You should maintain eye contact for about the length of a spoken phrase, then move on to someone else, again for the length of a phrase. This will be felt by your audience to be a natural and personal length of time, especially if it is coupled with a centred, calm speaking pace.

A good strategy when giving a presentation is to find a person on your left, on your right and in the middle of your audience to talk to. Deliver one phrase to the eye triangle of the person on your left, one to the right and one to the person in the middle. Keep going like this, then gradually make contact with more people until you get a good sense of your audience as a whole.

Eye contact starts at the feet

Presenters often give poor eye contact because their feet, when standing, are not placed symmetrically towards the audience. If your feet are parallel to one another or the toes of each foot are slightly turned away from each other, it is possible for the whole body, and therefore your eye contact, to turn equally from one side of the audience to another. If, however, one foot is turned in the same direction as the other, the whole body and sweep of the eyes will turn in the direction of the most outwardly turned foot.

Sight lines

It is good practice to check your sight lines in your presentation venue, before your audience arrives. Make sure that, wherever you may be sitting or standing to deliver your presentation, you can take in the whole audience using your peripheral vision. This should require minimal or no head turning. Stand or sit in as central a position as possible in relationship to where the audience will be sitting. If you find that it is not possible to take in the whole of the audience area, move backwards until you can. If possible, move the seating to achieve the same effect. This will give you a sense of taking control of your surroundings and will make you look more at home

ENERGY APPROPRIATE TO THE VENUE

Diligently using the methods in this book may well lead you to having a larger-than-life presence. Be careful! A larger-than-life presence may work in a 1000-seater theatre. The same presence in a small office or venue may blast people out of their seats and completely turn them off. Adjust your presence to suit the audience and venue.

GET TO KNOW YOUR AUDIENCE

When you are presenting, try to strike up a rapport with your audience before the session begins, for example over morning coffee. Apart from the usual conversation, this is an opportunity to gather useful information from participants or, where appropriate, to give them an outline of your presentation.

YOUR FRIENDS AND ALLIES IN THE AUDIENCE

It is worth remembering that the vast majority of any audience are on your side. They have come to be enriched, informed or entertained in one way or another. This fact was consciously used in nineteenth-century theatre and opera productions. The head of a theatre company would hire a group of distinguished-looking individuals – known as the **claque** – and 'plant' them throughout the audience. During the performance they would make appropriate noises of approval and would launch into generous and lusty applause, sparking the rest of the audience into an equally enthusiastic response.

In any audience there is already a claque waiting for you. The simple fact is that many people are natural smilers and nodders. These people are the members of your naturally occurring claque – all you have to do is notice and acknowledge them.

The identification of your claque can be carried out before you give your presentation. If your presentations are carried out in hotels, for example, you can sit in the lobby and be watch the people who are going to attend. When you begin to present, notice, using your peripheral vision, the natural smilers and nodders in your audience. Mark out three smilers and nodders — one to your left, one to your right and one in the centre. Address your first remarks to these three people.

With practice this will become second nature. You will be able to walk in, mark out your claque, acknowledge them with an almost invisible nod or smile and launch smoothly and easily into your presentation.

James Lawley, psychotherapist, management trainer and founding member of the Central London NLP Practice

I have used the idea of a claque in the audience on many occasions. I now make it a point to make contact with people as they arrive, preferably by talking personally to them or, if this is not possible, by welcoming them all. At the very least I try to make eye contact and smile. When I am being introduced before a presentation, I will seek out the people in the audience from whom I received the greatest response and attempt to acknowledge them with a smile or a nod. This helps me to create rapport and gives me a sense of connectedness with those individuals. I have found that if I consider these people to be 'light sources', radiating warmth to the people sitting immediately around them, my sense of connection expands during the presentation to include the whole audience.

FEEDBACK – ELECTRONIC AND PERSONAL

Reviewing your presentations frequently, even in small chunks, will help you pick up on those areas that are going well and those that need some work. You will become aware of those areas that you have omitted to cover. You might like to keep a note of these things in a notebook or on tape. Lay yourself open to inspiration.

The use of video cameras to record and review performance is a feature of many presentation skills courses. Cameras can be absolutely brutal in highlighting the areas where you need to do some more work but they also frequently highlight those areas in which you are unconsciously exceeding your own expectations. Valuable as video feedback is, however, it is impractical for day-to-day use.

For home use, or while out and about, a handheld tape recorder is a fine, inexpensive and portable alternative. If you prefer something of a very high digital quality, a mini-disc recorder is an excellent investment. The beauty of these voice recorders is that you can choose to move around or stand still as you present.

But I hate the sound of my voice on tape!

Just about everyone absolutely detests the sound of their recorded voice. Why does the voice that sounds so resonant inside your head sound so awful on the tape recorder? Accept and like yourself and your voice. Listen to some well-known TV and radio presenters. Do they all speak in a groomed, eloquent way? The medium is saturated with quirks, idiosyncrasies and speech impediments of every kind.

CHAPTER 6
Strategies and Techniques

The room was hushed,
The speaker mute,
He'd left his speech
In his other suit.

KENNETH MCFARLAND,
ELOQUENCE IN PUBLIC SPEAKING

Stand up, speak out and don't bump into the furniture.

NOEL COWARD

GENERATING YOUR CONTENT

Research over the past 30 years shows that the two sides of our brain function in different but complementary ways. The left cerebral hemisphere specializes in tasks of a more linear/verbal nature – arithmetic, grammar, logic etc. The right cerebral hemisphere, in contrast, specializes in more artistic or pattern based tasks – rhythm, texture, colour, pattern, shape etc. It is now widely acknowledged that we need the functions of both these hemispheres, working in harmony, to carry out even the simplest activities.

For example think of how you recognize an acquaintance. Recognizing their face is done by the pictorial right brain; remembering their name is a function of the verbal left brain. So what relevance does this have for writing a presentation?

RIGHT BRAIN: THE CREATIVE GENERATOR

For the purposes of constructing a presentation, think of the right cerebral hemisphere as the **creative generator** of the material that you wish to present, like a team of investigative and creative journalists. The left hemisphere is the editor/organizer who gives coherent shape to the apparent chaos of the day's breaking news. To the outside observer, the flow of journalists in and out of the building, or the flow of their phone calls, faxes and emails may look chaotic and disordered. Without further sorting the articles do not make a coherent newspaper. The flow of activity radiates out to the world and the gathered information floods back into the centre.

The biggest obstacle that many people face when writing a presentation is in trying to get it all down on paper in the correct logical sequence — beginning, middle and end — before the creative generator has been to work, i.e. before they have formulated all their raw ideas. Premature logical ordering of the material can create 'log jams' on the paper as you suddenly remember important points that you have left out. Frustration, the wastepaper bin and a desire to give it all up all start overflowing!

It is much easier first to let the right brain get to work on the task of generating material and then let the left brain structure it into a logical and understandable sequence. Write down *all* your ideas in a way that suits you, then start to structure them.

LEFT BRAIN: THE EDITOR/ORGANIZER

Having generated some ideas, you can now begin to order them into a linear and understandable sequence. Number each idea in order of priority. Now break down each idea into a key word or phrase. Use these as a prompt for your presentation.

Key words

Key words act like easily identifiable landmarks guiding you, the presenter, to your ultimate destination. These landmarks can liberate you from needing a verbatim text of your presentation. Presenters who use a series of key words end up with a better comprehension and memory of their material than those who slavishly stick to reading their material, word by word, from a text or script.

The speaker who simply reads out their presentation has to have their face and eyes pointing into the text most of the time, which reduces their visual impact and audibility. Evocative key words, on the other hand, directly push the presenter's memory buttons, allowing the speaker to keep their eyes and face pointing in the direction of the audience. This enhances their visual impact, makes their voice more audible and leads to a much more compelling presentation. Greater visual contact also allows a presenter to make a moment-by-moment assessment of how the audience is responding to the presentation and to adjust his or her behaviour accordingly.

Progress now

Break your presentation into key words and deliver it to an imaginary audience.

Index cards

A useful way of arranging your material is to write each key word down, in large capital letters, on the centre of an index card. You can place any additional instructions, e.g. 'pause and centre' or a smiley face reminding you to smile at the audience, on the side of the card.

Index cards are much less intrusive than the standard sheet of paper. They do not rattle loudly in your hand and show the audience how nervous you truly are! They can be held, virtually unnoticeably, at your side as you speak. They are also small enough to be kept in your pocket until required.

If left to their own devices, however, index cards have a nasty habit of rearranging themselves into a totally incomprehensible order, especially if you drop them in mid-presentation! For this reason it is a good idea to use a paper punch and treasury tags. Make a hole with the paper punch at the top left-hand corner of your index cards and thread the treasury tag through the holes. This will keep your precious notes in order through even the most demanding presentations.

WILL ANYONE REMEMBER YOU?

To ensure the best possible audience recall of your subject avoid, at all costs, delivering a presentation. Instead try delivering lots of little presentations, interspersed with related audience activities and breaks.

If you want your audience to remember what you have actually said, you will need to say it in a way that suits the natural peaks and troughs of the average person's attention span. Typically, people will recall more material from the beginning and end of a presentation and less from the middle. The longer a presentation is, without significant changes of style, the less you can expect your audience to remember.

Changes of style, audience involvement and breaks create more opportunities for greater total recall of your message.

STRUCTURING A PRESENTATION

A Texan revivalist preacher was asked for the secret of his great success. After thinking deeply for a few moments he gave the following reply:

First I tell them what I am going to say. Then I say it. And then I tell them what I have just said.

This is excellent advice that can be profitably used by any presenter. It has stood the test of time and is deservedly popular.

1 **Tell the audience what you are going to say**
Give them an outline of the content of your presentation. Make it simple — no more than three or four points, for example:

Good evening ladies and gentlemen (or other appropriate greeting). Tonight I am going to speak to you about F.M. Alexander and the history of his discoveries. I will then give a demonstration Alexander Technique lesson to a member of the audience. I will conclude my presentation by answering any questions that you may have.

2   Then say it

Deliver the content of your presentation, including demonstrations, questions and answers.

3   Tell them what you have just said

Conclude your presentation by summarizing your three or four key points. Thank your audience for their attendance. This will bring your presentation to a clean end and avoid that uncomfortable feeling of uncertainty that often accompanies poorly concluded presentations.

4   Next steps

Encourage your audience to follow up your presentation by offering them some next steps:

That concludes my presentation for this evening. Thank you for your attendance. For those of you who wish to find out more, there are leaflets on the table by the door . . . you may contact me at my office . . . I will remain in the room for another ten minutes. Please feel free to approach me.

Introductions: purpose, benefit and structure

A good system for introducing presentations is **PBS**: **Purpose, Benefit and Structure**. Here is an example from a talk that I recently gave on the Alexander Technique.

Purpose *Good evening ladies and gentlemen. My name is Alan Mars and tonight I have come to talk to you about the Alexander Technique.*

Benefits *As well as helping with bad backs, stiff necks and so on, the Alexander Technique is very useful for helping actors to control stage stress and to harness the 'buzz' factor during performance.*

Structure *First of all I will give you a short biography of F.M. Alexander and how he made his discoveries. Then I will do a few short demonstration lessons with members of the audience. And finally I will answer any questions that you may have.*

The PBS structure above has been set out in a fairly mechanical way for ease of instruction. For the actual delivery it can be a lot more fluid and conversational in feel.

The end: summary, conclusions and next steps

A good way to round off a presentation is through **SCN: Summary, Conclusions and Next Steps**.

Summary *So we've had the history of F.M. Alexander, we've done a hands on demonstration with some members of the audience and finally we had some very interesting questions.*

Conclusions *We've heard how the technique helped Alexander with his breathing problems on stage and we've seen how the technique improved the way our volunteers used their voice in a Shakespeare text. Please do keep practising the exercises — you'll get more acting jobs if you do.*

Next steps *For those of you who want to ask questions privately or who would like details of future training courses I will be in the room for another 15 minutes. Please feel free to approach me. My cards are on the table at the back.*

Both of the structuring formats above are extremely clear and easy to follow. They may seem somewhat rigid but, as with any technique, easy practice makes for an easier, and more natural-sounding, delivery.

CHERYL WINTER

Cheryl Winter FCIPD is an Abbey National trainer and freelance training consultant

CW: In my 15 years of training I am constantly amazed by how many people give me a gift each time I sit in a presentation, training session or even a meeting. And the more I place myself in these situations the more I learn about the art of motivation – to motivate is to get people to do something they want to do. As I watch and listen to presenters, managers or trainers I am always moved to do at least one new thing the next time I am faced with a group of people. So when asked to present my key tip or skill, I chose one which helps me to prepare presentations, training sessions or even a three-day event. It is one which I learnt in my early days of selling mortgages and life assurance and from the days of sales training. It is a set of steps which helped me both sell to my customers and train trainers.

I went through these steps whenever I needed to sell a customer a mortgage which they could actually get from any financial outlet. First I read up on my client: where they worked, accounts already held, and whether I had ever seen them before. Then when we sat down together, I would confirm that this was a mortgage interview. I would tell them what the benefits would be for them, such as competitive rates and personal service throughout, and then I would set out the sort of things we might need to discuss. As the meeting progressed, I would summarize the financial data, then towards the end I would do a summary of what they had told me and what I had covered. My grand finale would be to present them with the personal package of the perfect mortgage – and then look at what we could do to get the ball rolling.

A few years later, as I managed my first ever training team, I attempted to put together an event on how to get your message across – and ensure the delegates on the course were passionate and excited – when it was only 9.05 a.m. and the subject was accident and sickness insurance! As I thought and planned and looked for examples to show my new trainers, a colleague asked me for some coaching on how to do a mortgage interview. As I started to coach her I realized that exactly the same technique would work for presentations:

1 First I read up on my client: where they worked, accounts already held, and whether I had ever seen them before.

Preparation – What do you know about your audience that you could bring into your presentation to show them you really do care about how much they get out of it?

2 I would confirm that this was a mortgage interview.

Topic – Be clear and concise about the subject matter of your presentation.

3 I would tell them what the benefits would be for them . . .

Motive – Why should your audience bother to pay attention to you? What will they personally get out of your presentation? Some of them could be giving up their lunch or an important meeting or be at the end of a very hard day – make them want to be there emotionally. Use a statement which will link your presentation to their job, their company or their industry, or find a common theme to make your motive really emotional.

4 . . . and then I would set out the sort of things we might need to discuss.

Structure – Let the audience know concisely and clearly what you will be covering.

5 As the meeting progressed, I would summarize the financial data . . .

The topic – The work you do on the structure of your presentation and your use of language will take you a long way towards moving your audience.

6 . . . towards the end I would do a summary of what they had told me and what I had covered . . .

Summary – Remind them of where they have been by revisiting your topic headings. This is a point at which presenters sometimes try to add more information – take great care, for as you start to summarize members of your audience will take it as a signal that you have covered everything and will start to switch off. Don't add new data or great findings here – they will fall on inattentive ears.

7 My grand finale would be to present them with the personal package of the perfect mortgage . . .

Findings – Summarize your own views on the subject, or any conclusions you'd like the audience to ponder as they prepare to leave.

8 . . . and then look at what we could do to get the ball rolling.

Move on – What can your audience do to get more of what you have told them?

BRIBERY – WITHOUT THE CORRUPTION

Leave nothing to chance. Don't live in doubt about the outcome of your presentations. **Bribe** your audience.

B – Begin positively and powerfully

- Make full use of posture, voice and personal space.
- Give an overview of your presentation.

R – Repeat your main points

- In varying ways, repeat them at least three times.

I – Involve your audience

- Use current events, questions and multi-sensory language.

B – Be creative

- Use stories, comparisons and alliteration.

E – End positively and powerfully

- Make full use of posture, voice and personal space.
- Make a short summary of your presentation.
- Conclude clearly and powerfully.

Progress now

B – Begin positively and powerfully

- Use **posture**, centring and your voice.

- Give an **overview** of your presentation.

- Remember that audience recall is at its peak at the beginning and end of a presentation, so make it count.

R – Repeat your main points

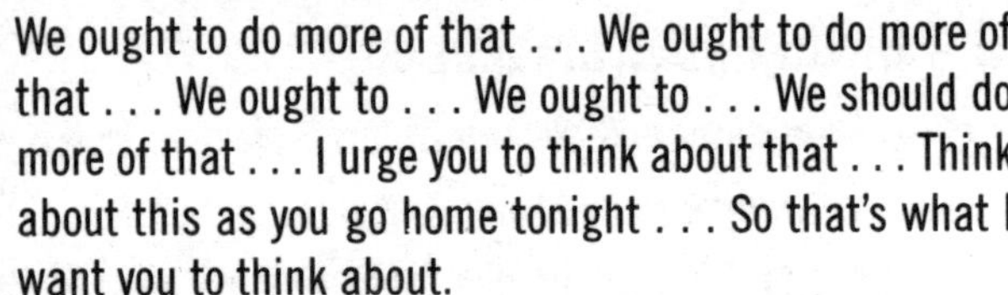

The above quotes are from **Bill Clinton**'s keynote speech 'The Struggle for the Soul of the Twenty-first Century'. In this speech Clinton took a long hard look at the positive and negative aspects of where the major Western powers had come from, where they were now and the possible futures. The speech looked at the hard realities that we all will have to face. It also celebrated real, life-enhancing progress in business, health, education and human rights. And he asked everyone to consider the significant difficulties and opportunities that almost certainly lay ahead for ourselves and for future generations. Each time he repeated or varied one of the above phrases, he drove his message home. The speech was global and covered past, present and future but much of the time came down to simple, common-sense recommendations.

Progress now

I – Involve your audience

- Use **audience involvement** and activities where you break into groups or pairs.

- KISS – Keep it **short and sweet**! Audience involvement works best when the audience is awake. Reading your presentation aloud from a script will take about twice as long as reading it silently. Presenting it to an audience will take about twice as long again. Time it in advance with a friend or colleague!

- Whenever possible or appropriate use **inclusive language** – 'we', 'us' and 'our'.

- Use **questions** – rhetorical and Q&A sessions.

- Use **multi-sensory language**. People think differently: some are predominantly visual thinkers while others are more auditory or feeling.

- Use references to **current events** where appropriate.

Progress now

B – Be creative

- Use **illustrative stories** and anecdotes with different times, places, characters, events and objects.

- Use **comparisons** – a good way to present statistical information.

- Introduce **alliteration** – 'Short, sharp shock'; 'Right customer, right product, right time.'

Progress now

E – End positively and powerfully

- Use your **posture, voice** and **personal space**.
- Make a short **summary** of your presentation and outline next steps.
- Conclude **clearly and powerfully**.

STYLE

Many presenters, teachers and lecturers have a habit of communicating their material in an overly verbal and linear way. This attempt to convey maximum information is done with the best of intentions but the presenter on this path may, sadly, send 75 per cent of their audience to sleep, as even the most linear and logical person thinks in a rich and colourful way:

1   In pictures – large and **small** . . . still pictures . . . moving pictures . . . in black and white . . . in colour . . . in a variety of shades. Many people have a personal vision. Certain groups share a vision.

2   In words and sentences – in different tones of voice . . . *fast* and s l o w . . . **LOUDLY**!!! and quietly in just the same way as they speak in different tones, speeds and volumes.

3   With feelings and emotions – gut feelings . . . feelings of commitment . . . heartfelt feelings . . .

4   With sensations, movements and qualities – smooth . . . rough . . . silky . . . light . . . **heavy** . . .

Most people use, to a greater or lesser degree, a combination of visual, auditory, tactile and feeling/emotional thinking. Audiences respond to your words, voice and actions with their own unique combination of multi-sensory thought associations.

An overly linear presentation may plunge your audience into boredom. They will try to escape from this physically unpleasant state through mind wandering, while the more conscientious members of your audience will try to 'concentrate' on what you are saying.

The job of a presenter is to magically evoke pictures, sounds and feelings in full, three-dimensional colour within the brains of the audience. The more pictures, colour, tone, texture and feeling quality in your presentation, the greater your audience's engagement and recall will be and the more they will be inspired, moved or motivated. The next few exercises will increase the sensory richness conveyed by your speech and gestures.

Air Sculptures

Most people spontaneously paint or sculpt pictures in the air with their hands and arms during the course of an absorbing conversation. For some people, the unfamiliarity or tension of a formal presentation can interfere with this natural ability. Other people continue sculpting the air but fail to amplify their gestures enough to take account of the needs of a larger group.

Dave is a representative of a firm that specializes in alternative holidays. He started a presentation by describing a beautiful holiday island:

'*The sea is blue and usually very still. The beaches are beautiful and very clean. In the late afternoons there are classes in yoga.*'

This had very little impact on the group as they felt that he had just read a beautiful but uncompelling list.

As he continued, he began to use gesture more expansively:

'*Imagine a perfectly still, mirror-like blue sea* (Dave made a smooth, round, horizontal gesture indicating the still mirror-like quality) *spread out in front of you* (Dave spread his arms out wide and gazes to the sea's horizon). *You lie down and relax on the golden sands* (made a reclining gesture with his hands and changed to present tense). *Later on you do some nice relaxing yoga* (Dave did a combined yoga stretch and yawn).'

As Dave spoke this time, his voice took on a much more relaxing and hypnotic quality. Everyone agreed that his presentation was more compelling and relaxing.

Perhaps one of the most interesting points that the above examples draw out is the connection between voice and movement. Making gestures that congruently reflect your words and meaning will always enhance the impact of your voice.

Progress now

Directions

1 The next time you see someone asking a local person for directions, watch how centred and attentive the local person is to the newcomer. Notice how they indicate left, right and straight ahead. How do you know when they are describing a significant landmark? How expansive and clear are the gestures? Does the tone of voice vary with the gestures? Do they maintain eye contact and adjust the pace of their speech to match the assimilation speed of the newcomer?

2   Try giving clear, well-paced directions to an imaginary stranger. If it makes it easier you can first practise the visual, vocal and verbal aspects of the directions separately then combine them. Feel free to amplify the elements more than you normally would.

3   Now apply the same skills to a small chunk of your presentation and see the difference they make.

Going over the top

Some people object that the air sculpture exercise makes them feel as if their behaviour while presenting is over the top, but invariably their listeners report a perfectly pitched presentation. When the session is played back on video the presenter is usually pleasantly surprised. The few occasions when a presenter truly goes over the top are still useful as it stretches their boundaries and makes available a much wider area of middle-ground choices.

Air sculptures and voice work connect you more fully with your audience. With your words you speak to their mind while your posture and gestures paint compelling images in the space that hovers between presenter and audience.

MOVING EFFECTIVELY ON STAGE

Many presenters have times when they have to speak and move simultaneously: moving from one side of the stage to another to spread your attention to different sections of a large audience or to reach different items of professional equipment.

It is quite appropriate for a presenter to continue talking to the audience as he or she moves from one location to the other. Many presenters' method of moving is, however, highly inappropriate, for example turning to face the object that they are walking towards and presenting their side profile or, even worse, their back to the audience. There are many problems associated with this way of moving:

1   Maximum visual presence is associated with 'full frontal' posture. The side view is much less impactful for the audience.

2   If you fully face one side of the stage you will have fully turned your back to the opposite side of the audience.

3   If you face the back of the stage you will have literally and metaphorically turned your back on the audience.

The stage walk

The stage walk is an excellent way of avoiding movement problems. It comprises a series of sideways, cross-over steps which help you to keep more of the front of your body facing the auditorium. It will probably feel a bit unfamiliar and crab-like at first. With practice it becomes flowing and easy and ensures that you communicate with maximum visual, vocal and verbal impact.

Progress now

1   Pause and centre yourself. Scan the room using your full peripheral vision.

2   Practise crossing from one side of a room to the other by crossing your left foot in front of your right foot.

3   Now try it with your right foot crossing in front of your left, with the left foot crossing behind the right, then with right behind left.

4   Now try using different combinations of the above steps.

5   Do the stage walk as you recite a piece of poetry or a nursery rhyme.

Presenters who habitually bump into the furniture will find that they will become much more confident and assured in their movement if they practise using their peripheral vision as they move.

You are unlikely, even with practice, to walk in an absolutely straight line from one side of the room to another. You are much more likely to walk in gently curving lines. When you are addressing a group of listeners you will be able to select a curving stage walk that will be most suitable for the seating arrangements of the particular venue in which you are working.

Walking backwards

Master the art of walking backwards while continuing to face the audience.

Progress now

1   Arrange two or three pieces of furniture to represent pieces of equipment, such as flip charts, that you might use while speaking.

2   Move to the front of the room, pause and centre yourself. Expand your field of peripheral vision.

3   Briefly glance over your shoulder at the equipment. Look forward again.

4   Gently walk backwards until you are standing beside the equipment.

5   Repeat this until it becomes easy and familiar.

6   Now try walking backwards while reciting some poetry or a nursery rhyme.

7   Rehearse the walk as part of your presentation, with a mental picture of the venue.

THE STAGE WALK AND ADRENALINE CONTROL

During one management training course I worked with a bank executive who delivered a presentation on life insurance. He was wonderfully enthusiastic and excited about his subject. Unfortunately his enthusiasm resulted in him walking round in circles as he talked. The more enthusiastic he became, the faster he walked. Faster walking led to faster talking and he became very red in the face. His non-verbal behaviour was so powerful that it literally made some people dizzy. Very few people were able to keep track of what he was saying. There was so much adrenalin coursing around his system that he felt even more tense when asked to stand still while speaking.

Practising the flowing, gentle and predictable curve of the stage walk allowed him to channel his adrenaline without suppressing it. His face changed back to his normal colouring. The added eye contact with his listeners encouraged him to slow down his speech to an understandable pace. As he continued to practise, his movements became more precise and graceful. This not only made him calmer but also allowed the audience to share some of his enthusiasm for his subject.

SPATIAL MARKING AND ANCHORING

Spatial marking is a way of using non-verbal behaviour to increase audience understanding, comprehension and recall of the subject on which you are speaking.

One of the commonest and simplest methods of marking out points of information in space and time is to be found in the expression:

'In the first place . . .'

the speaker makes their first point

'. . . and in the second place . . .'

the speaker makes their second point

'. . . and thirdly and finally . . .'

The speaker will frequently extend their thumb for the first place, their index finger for the second place and their middle finger for the final point.

The origins of the expression 'In the first place . . .' stretch back to the days of classical Greek oratory. The oratory competitions required the speakers to deliver enormously long speeches from memory — too long for the average memory — so the orators had to use memory triggers. One section of their address would be practised and memorized in a certain place, for example by a fountain, the next section on the steps of the judicial buildings and the following section by the senate house. When the orator delivered their address they would visualize each location and thus recall each section of their speech in turn. This process was, over time, accompanied by the expression 'In the first place . . . .'. The repeated use of this expression caused it to become a memory and orientation trigger not only for the speakers but also for the listeners.

Timelines

People understand time as having a quality of direction. One commonly understood timeline flows from the back — past — to the front — future. Consider expressions such as 'That's all behind me now', referring to a past event, or 'I see a bright future ahead for this student', implying a forwards direction to future events.

Another frequently used timeline is one that runs from left — the past — to right — the future, for example in 'before and after' photographs in adverts. By marking out specific points in a line that runs from the audience's left to the audience's right you can emphasize important points non-verbally as well as verbally.

Progress now

Practise creating a left–right timeline with some material that you have to present.

1 Choose three main points that you would like to emphasize, or mark out the beginning, middle and end of your presentation.

2 Stand in the middle of an imaginary presentation space. Remember to pause and centre yourself.

3 Introduce yourself to the imaginary audience and then move to the:

   a) right of stage (audience left) for the first point, e.g. *'A high-fibre diet is good for your health.'*

   b) centre stage for the following point, e.g. *'Dietary fibre is found in fruit and vegetables.'*

   c) left of stage (audience right) for the final point, e.g. *'Be healthy! Eat more fruit and vegetables!'*

4 Practise going through the whole procedure more minimally by standing still and gesturing with your:

   a) right hand (audience left) for the first point

   b) both hands for the next point

   c) left hand for the final point.

Spatial marking in business

The regional director of a high street banking chain addresses a group of area managers on how the bank has been developing up to the present day and its possible direction over the next ten years. He stands in the centre of the speaking area, introduces himself and welcomes the managers to his talk. He then moves:

two paces to audience left
'Today I will talk about where we have come from'

back to centre stage
'where the bank is in today's marketplace'

two paces to audience right
'and finally I will talk about my vision for our future'

By doing this he has neatly structured his presentation both verbally and non-verbally. He has used his stage walk so that his voice is clear and his visual presence is strong. While moving he has visually swept the room and addressed his first three remarks to 'allies' within the audience.

The director then returns to the centre of the room and pauses for a couple of seconds to clear the slate for the main body of his talk. He then delivers each section of his presentation from the appropriate point on the stage. Audience attention and comprehension is kept high as they know, unconsciously, with each shift the director makes exactly where they are in the presentation.

The director concludes his presentation by standing centre stage and marking out his three points with hand gestures and eye directions:

'And to conclude my presentation'

gestures with right hand to audience left
'this is where we have come from'

both hands gesture towards mid-line
'this is our position today'

left hand to audience right
'and a golden future lies ahead!'

THE POWER OF COMMUNICATION

'There has been an upturn of confidence in the markets.'

'You're on shaky ground there.'

'The speech struck a chord with the public.'

'I smell a rat.'

'Let me chew it over for a while.'

'Keep in touch.'

'It was a very touching gesture.'

Some recent research gave an account of how people responded to different words. Words with a more visual nature, for example, elicited more activity in the brain's visual cortex. Words with a more auditory character tended to elicit more activity in the parts of the brain that processed auditory information. It therefore makes sense to use as wide a range of sensory words as possible to pull in the majority of an average audience.

There is no such thing as a single sense thinker. Everyone uses a variety of senses. By using a variety of sensory words, it is possible not only to build rapport with more of the audience but also to gain a deeper, unconscious rapport with each individual.

1   Light up your own brain first. Become sensorily associated with your material by using clear and motivating metaphors. When you present, you will be brighter and firing on all cylinders.

2   Start with feeling (slower) words, then move to (faster) visual words.

3   There are times when audiences are more than fully engaged, such as meetings where people are upset and angry. The use of fewer sensory and more emotionally neutral words can be extremely useful to help to calm such an atmosphere but only if you have acknowledged how your audience is feeling, otherwise you run the risk of being perceived as cold and uncaring.

CHAPTER 7
Practicalities

Whenever you are asked if you can do a job, tell 'em 'Certainly I can!' Then get busy and find out how to do it.

THEODORE ROOSEVELT

Practice is the best of all instructors.

PUBLIUS SYRUS

DEVELOPING 'NOUS'

The word 'nous' means a kind of inbuilt knowledge — an unconscious competence or know-how. The information in this chapter will help to get in touch with your nous — your native wisdom of presenting.

- Listen to presentations given by your colleagues and other presenters on the same and other subjects. They may have an interesting and refreshingly different slant on presenting the same material.

- Attend conferences in your own field/s of interest. This will give you the opportunity to study other presentations and will keep you at the sharp edge of your professional skills.

- Keep up to speed by reading professional journals, magazines and websites. Read the newspapers and keep clippings of interesting and topical articles. Use a good search engine to locate web pages on your subject. Search the growing number of quote sites on the internet for punchy quotes.

- Consider speaking at conferences and writing articles on your field of interest. This keeps your presence in the minds of others. Also, there is nothing like being in the firing line to keep you on your professional toes!

- Learn from the people to whom you present — they are quite possibly the best teachers you will ever have.

PRESENTATION STYLES

In order to choose the right style that will fit both you and your audience you will need to do your research and become familiar with the needs, preoccupation and expectations of your audience. Some of the categories below will help you to think through your presentation more thoroughly and tailor it to fit your audience more comfortably.

Formal or informal?

This is more a question of style than of content or structure. The informal style is closer in quality to a conversational feel. It is more likely to have questions and clarifications included in the body of the presentation. The formal presentation is closer in quality to a public speaking style. Formality implies roles, which can create more emotional distance. This distance is bridged by a larger-than-life performance style. Many gifted public speakers and presenters have mastered the more intimate informal style even in the most formal, structured settings while speaking to large audiences.

Large or small?

Larger presentations require greater elements of performance, entertainment and audience stimulation within them. Because they generally involve less audience interaction, they tend to be more structured and formal. The smaller presentation, even when formal, tends to be more conversational and in a lower key — you do not want to blast your audience against the wall with a too-powerful delivery.

Tell or sell?

Are you seeking simply to inform your audience or do you want to get them to buy into an idea? An informative 'tell' presentation is based around conveying factual information, for example at annual general meetings or induction training. A 'sell' presentation will tend to concentrate more on getting the board, the committee, the members, the staff or the audience to buy into an idea, a policy or a course of action. It could use fear and apprehension — the stick — to get people to avoid moving in a certain direction. Or, more constructively, it can use inspiration and excitement — the carrot — to get people to move positively in a certain direction.

Mixing sell and tell

While a treasurer's report, for example, may be predominantly factual and informative, it should still have some of the colour, verve and personal touch associated with sell presentations. It usually benefits from some sell to finish off:

'The organization has done very badly this year. We really need to get our act together and increase profits' or *'What a fantastic year it has been. If we keep going this way next year will be even better.'*

Participative

The participative presentation is usually set up in the style of 'tell' – the presenter or facilitator will set out the goals and objectives to be achieved or the agenda to be followed. In this situation the audience gets involved in the action. The topics are discussed in a more spontaneous fashion or in a more formal, ordered fashion with audience members airing their views in sequence. The presenter may summarize the topics at the end of the meeting and set out any conclusions the group has reached.

Coaching and training

These presentations are based around imparting skills to or drawing out skills from the audience and tend to be delivered to smaller audiences.

Usually the trainer will give a background or history to the skill being studied. The trainer will then do a demonstration, often with a member of the audience, of the first few steps of the skill to be acquired. Once the skill has been explained and demonstrated, the group will then practise the new skills individually or in smaller groups. The trainer will present to the individual or groups in a more instructive coaching style until the new skill begins to click. The whole group will then reconvene and the presenter will talk through and demonstrate a new layer of sub-skills. The demonstration will usually incorporate questions, queries and clarifications from the practice and coaching section. In this way, layer by layer, a new skill set is developed by the group.

At the end of the course, and often at the end of each sub-section, the trainer will summarize previous steps, draw conclusions and make recommendations for future practice.

Internal or external?

Presenting to an internal audience is a bit like interacting with your family. There may be politics involved. There will be those with whom you have closer alliances and those with whom friction occurs more readily. Internal audiences tend to be less formal but it is a good idea to anticipate the objections and support you might reasonably expect to receive from various quarters. Although you have a role and job description within the organization, people have personal responses to you.

When you are presenting externally you are functioning as a representative of your organization or a representative of the ideas, products and services that you are wishing to sell. You will be perceived relatively less personally and relatively more as the role you represent.

USE OF VISUAL AIDS

Often presenters think that a presentation *is* the visual aids that they use – the PowerPoint, the overhead projection, the slide show – and that their part in this presentation is simply to supply a voice-over to the visuals. Often the psychology behind this approach is based on fear and on wanting to hide away. Remember that the best visual aids you have are your own body language, composure and knowledge of the subject. So ask yourself 'Is this visual aid really necessary? Would my presentation really suffer without it?' If you find yourself honestly answering 'no' to this question then have the courage of your convictions and leave it out. If the answer is 'yes', then read on. The section below will provide some valuable tips for the best possible use of visual aids.

Visibility and clarity

For something to be a visual aid rather than a visual hurdle you must ask yourself:

- Can my visual aid be seen easily and clearly from all parts of the room?
- Is it simple, spare and easily understood?

Visual aid or handout?

Often a lot of material which is displayed on projectors – long quotes, complex graphs and figures – would be better given as a handout. Cut out or simplify what you put on the projector and tell your audience that you will be providing additional information in the form of a handout at the end of your presentation. Do not give handouts at the beginning – your audience are only human and many of them will read the handout rather than looking at or listening to you.

Non-verbal relationship to visual aids

Look, point, look back and speak . . .

When speakers are using a visual aid there is a powerful tendency to look at it while speaking rather than looking at the audience. Not only does this reduce the speaker's visual impact, it also reduces their audibility. In most cases the speaker does not actually have to use the visual aid for their memory – it is to aid audience comprehension and recall. So:

1   Pause silently and **look** at the visual aid.

2   **Point** at the section to which you are referring.

3   **Look back** to the audience.

4   Finally, **speak** to the audience.

You could extend this attitude to all of the procedures you carry out on stage. The simplest activity carried out in an unco-ordinated way can induce discomfort in both audience and presenter. Communicate comfort and ease by practising writing on the flipchart, changing slides and switching projectors on and off with mind and body co-ordination.

For presentations where the venue itself is supplying the equipment, phone or write beforehand to make sure that they have everything you will need. If possible get there the day before to physically check for yourself and to rehearse.

Low-tech longevity – the perennial flipchart

Why has the flipchart, the lowest-tech of visual aids, remained popular for such a long time? For a start, because it is low-tech, there is less likely to go wrong with it. Flipcharts can be prepared in advance or they can be used to facilitate the here-and-now process of a presentation or training session. As well as writing on the flipchart you can draw illustrative diagrams and pictures.

- If you prepare your flipcharts before you arrive at the venue, make sure you have a way of transporting them so that they arrive in pristine condition. If you roll them up, take something to keep them flat when they are rolled out again.

- Practise writing on a flipchart until it becomes at least as clear as your normal writing.

- Practise drawing any graphs, illustrations or pictures on the flipchart. Prepare these drawings beforehand or get someone else with good graphic skills to prepare them for you.

- Check that your presentation venue has flipchart pens, flipchart paper and blu-tack available.

- Take a spare set of pens with you – even if the venue has them they may not be working properly.

- Use clearly visible colours – blacks, blues, darker reds and greens. Yellows and oranges can sometimes be difficult to read. Pinks can be distracting.

- For more formal presentations, leave a blank sheet of paper between each written one, as the writing from the previous sheet tends to show through. This is less important for informal presentations, training sessions or meetings.

- Use both upper case and lower case – using upper case only can make it difficult to read.

- <u>Underlining</u> can be useful for headings and important points.

- Some flipchart pens have bladed tips – the thick edge can give a bold effect.

Projectors

For more formal or larger presentations, a projector can be very useful. As well as being larger than a flipchart, the image position on the screen or wall can be adjusted to give maximum visibility for everyone present.

- **Make sure that you have a spare bulb!** This is the most common cause of mechanical failure of all projectors, ancient or modern.

- **Know your machine.** How long does it take to warm up? Can you operate it without fumbling about? What kind of screen does it need?

- **Buy an extension lead.** A purchase worth its weight in gold – projector leads are often short and power points are often in inconvenient places. The extension lead will give you more choices about setting up the presentation room for maximum comfort and effect.

- **Buy a remote or a handheld mouse if you use a laptop.** Using the touchpad or a mat-bound mouse will have you bobbing up and down during your presentation. This will muffle your visual and vocal impact. A remote or handheld mouse will free your eyes and voice to attend to the audience and will allow you to move more freely as you talk.

- **Buy a small but powerful pair of computer speakers.** If you use sound, especially in larger spaces, they will give a much louder, fuller sound than the speakers on your laptop.

- **Take a plain white sheet and drawing pins.** They will serve as a screen if there is nothing else available.

Popular programs – go easy

Certain presentation programs have become a victim of their own popularity and of overuse. Even when electronic presentations are done cleverly and potentially entertainingly, they lose the audience's attention because they have become used to them. When it comes to presentations, you can't beat human contact. Mix your slides judiciously with stories from your and others' personal experiences, use demonstrations and get your audience as active and involved as possible. Within this context your slides will make much more impact.

Preparing slides

A small critique of some presenters – they just love to cram their slides to bursting point. Let's not confuse quantity with quality.

Clear all the distraction off the slides and have either:

Three bullets down with five words across

- Blah Blah Blah Blah Blah
- Blah Blah Blah Blah Blah
- Blah Blah Blah Blah Blah

OR

Five bullets down with three words across

- Blah Blah Blah
- Blah Blah Blah
- Blah Blah Blah
- Blah Blah Blah
- Blah Blah Blah

Any more than that and the audience will be reading the slides rather than listening to you.

The T-shirt theory (less is more)

How many words can you get on a T-shirt and still make sure it is readable to a passer-by? Slides should be the same — visual, aesthetic and minimalist.

- Clear the clutter by removing company logos and repetitive headings from every slide — using them at the beginning and end will be quite sufficient.

- Use simple or familiar fonts that are easy to read:

  A sans serif font is easier to read than something fancy like this. Times New Roman is a familiar newspaper font. A mix of Upper Case and Lower Case is easier to read THAN CONSTANT CAPITALS. **Use bold text for added effect.** *Use italics and underlining <u>sparingly</u>.*

- Add a bit of colour — but not so much that it becomes a distraction.

- Get sumone to check your speling for oblivious and sutble misteaks!

Check your sequence once, twice and thrice

Check the sequence of acetates, slides and PowerPoint slides repeatedly. They have a mind of their own and like to come out at night and swap places.

Make sure that computer presentations are backed up on disc. Personal computers are still notorious for crashing. Computer gremlins have a wicked sense of humour and will save the most serious technical hitches for the most inconvenient and embarrassing moments. Post your most important files to yourself at a web-based email address so that they will be ready to download at your convenience anywhere that you have an internet connection.

Microphones and PA systems

Avoid using amplification except when absolutely necessary. Use the voice exercises in Chapter 6 to enhance your audibility instead.

- The types of situation where you may need to use a microphone are at conferences or large public meetings. The acoustics vary tremendously so get there early and do an audibility check with a friend or colleague.

- A cordless collar microphone is preferable to a fixed microphone and will allow you to move around.

- If you have never heard your voice amplified before, it can be a bit of a shock. Rehearse thoroughly with a microphone.

- If you have to use a fixed microphone, adjust it upwards or downwards until it is about six inches away from your mouth. Avoid pushing your mouth any closer to the microphone. It is particularly important to do a comparative sound check in situations where one presenter follows another — especially if the previous speaker has a much louder or softer voice than you.

- Public address systems have a tendency to make odd noises or to cut out. Check all of this out and, if necessary, make sure it is fixed in time for your presentation.

PREPARING THE ROOM

This section assumes that you have a reasonable degree of control over the environment in which you will be presenting. It ends by making a few suggestions about what to do if you have a potentially poor environment. Get to your venue in advance and check it thoroughly.

Accessibility

This is an extremely important factor if you are booking and organizing the event yourself. Consider public transport links, car parking and access for people with disabilities. For longer events also consider the local availability of decent overnight accommodation that will suit all budgets.

Room availability

Check beforehand that the room is actually available. If possible get a written acknowledgement of this. Do you need break out rooms for certain sessions? Check that they are also available and booked.

Room size

Is the room large enough for the expected size of audience? Will they be packed in like sardines or feel dwarfed and alienated by the size of the venue? Try to get the right balance between the anticipated size of your audience and the room available.

Seating arrangements and furniture

- Appropriate comfort is again the key. Look for upright chairs with shoulder and leg room.

- For larger audiences, theatre-style rows are the most convenient method of seating. For audiences of 20 and under, consider a horseshoe arrangements of chairs.

- Unless there is a lot of writing or note taking to be done avoid having tables in front of the audience's chairs or your chair, as they get in the way of activities you may have planned and create an emotional barrier between presenter and audience.

- For audiences of up to 100, where there is a fair amount of individual, partner or small group activity involved, consider presenting in the round for some of the time. Start off with the audience seated theatre style. When it comes to break-out time, ask them to move their chairs to the edge of the room to create more space — a wonderful way to get audience activity and participation started. When you come back to whole group activity, you can present from the middle of the room. Your voice and body language will need to be sufficiently strong to deal with this. If you are using your voice effectively you should be just as audible to the people behind you as to those in front and to the sides of you. You will, however, need to rotate slowly, like the beam from a lighthouse, to give everyone sufficient visual contact with you. You also have the option of standing, along with everyone else, at the perimeter of the circle and presenting from there. For participatory, training and celebratory events, presenting in the round is one of the most powerful tools for dissolving the barriers between presenter and audience.

For smaller meetings the round table, although not always readily available, is much less confrontational in style than the square or rectangular elements. Given that round tables are not that common, get to the meeting early enough to get the seat of your choice with maximum visibility and audibility.

Lighting

- Know where the light switches are! There will usually be more than one light in each room. Switch them on and off. Keep experimenting and adjusting until you get the most consistent spread of light.

- Windowless rooms or rooms with fluorescent lighting sap energy and consequently audience attention spans. Wherever possible, give your presentations in a room with windows and good natural lighting or with non-fluorescent light sources.

- Go and sit where the audience will be sitting and check that there will be no glaring lights shining into their eyes from where you, the presenter, will be standing. Avoid standing or sitting with your back to a window — especially when the sun is shining directly through it and into the eyes of the audience.

Acoustics

Some environments seem to absorb sound like a sponge — there are often lots of soft furnishings, thick carpets and curtains in these settings. Other environments reflect and echo sound more readily. These are often places with a lot of hard surroundings — concrete, glass, metal — and they can become noisy too easily.

- 🞤 Get to your venue early and do a sound check, whether you are being amplified or not. If your voice needs more power, do not simply try to speak louder. Centre yourself and imagine that you are singing as you speak. In addition to bringing out more dynamic variation in your voice, this will also bring out some of the higher, more carrying frequencies. A small stage — as little as 30 cm higher than floor level — can make the world of difference to your audibility.

- 🞤 Make eye contact! If you can focus on your audience, they will probably hear you.

Atmosphere, ventilation and temperature

Air is brain fuel — make sure there is sufficient ventilation. Familiarize yourself with the heating and air conditioning systems in the room. Be prepared to use the doors and windows judiciously. Check verbally with your audience, by asking if the temperature is suitable, and non-verbally — are they drooping, nodding off, fanning themselves, shivering? If in doubt go for a slightly cooler atmosphere and keep them warm and attentive by having activity and audience participation breaks more often.

Harsh or tedious environments can be softened or enlivened with flowers, plants and topic-related posters.

Refreshments

Coffee and tea are commonly supplied as refreshments in business environments. Herbal teas and bottled water are becoming increasingly available. Of all the drinks available, water is absolutely the most essential brain fuel available: it aids thinking, concentration and intellectual ability. Consider also adding fresh fruit to your afternoon and morning breaks as well as biscuits.

Toilet facilities

It doesn't matter how good a presenter you are . . . you simply cannot compete with that kind of discomfort. Make sure that toilet facilities are available nearby!

CHAPTER 8
Feedback

Learning is not compulsory – neither is survival.

W. EDWARDS DEMMING

The meaning of your communication is the response you get.
Keep adjusting your communication until you get the response that you desire.

JOHN GRINDER AND RICHARD BANDLER

HOW DID YOU DO?

You know your material inside out, back to front and left, right and centre. This gives you the control that allows you to track and read the audience. You can afford to deconstruct and reconstruct your presentation for them as you go along.

Before you reach this level of simultaneous output and feedback you will need to spend time on a more sequential mode of feedback – you do your presentation then you receive feedback from various sources. You should take notice from this feedback of the areas where you need further development and work, and acknowledge and reinforce your areas of excellence and strength. Rehearse your chosen areas for development and implement these improvements in future presentations.

Nowadays many businesses use some type of questionnaire to elicit specific feedback from clients, customers or audience. Think of the places where you have seen them – hotels, restaurants, conferences, training sessions and so on. The forms are usually split into several categories which, added together, give full and complete feedback on the session or service being provided. Each category is scored for quality or satisfaction, for example:

Excellent   Good   Average   Poor   Very poor

Other possibilities are a percentage for each category, with 100 per cent being equivalent to the peak of excellence and zero per cent equivalent to poorest of the poor. If you intend to become a great presenter you should be aiming to consistently score 85 per cent and above or for most of your scores to be in the 'excellent' category.

Who is it that decides what is good or poor when you are giving a presentation? The audience does. And so do you. It is also extremely helpful to have a close but objective friend or colleague to sit in as an observer at your presentations. This will take care of feedback from first, second and third positions.

Dr Brent Young, professor at the Imperial College of Science, Technology and Medicine, noticed a pattern of feedback emerging. Out of a class of students he consistently found that, while the vast majority of the class scored him highly, at the end of the academic year two or three students would assess him poorly.

He dealt with this in the first class of the year by telling the students that in the assessments at the end of the academic year he was highly rated by 97 per cent of his students. He then went on to say 'and for the two or three of you here who are going to think that I am a complete ___________, I apologise in advance!'

He set the expectations for learning and fun high and was also gracious enough to let people dislike him.

EVOLVING YOUR OWN FEEDBACK FORM

Below is a sample feedback form that you could use or adapt for your own purposes and circumstances:

How would you rate the presentation overall?

Excellent ☐ Good ☐ Average ☐ Poor ☐ Very poor ☐

What points worked well? What needs developing?

How would you rate the presenter's body language?

Excellent ☐ Good ☐ Average ☐ Poor ☐ Very poor ☐

What points worked well? What needs developing?

How would you rate the presenter's use of the voice?

Excellent ☐ Good ☐ Average ☐ Poor ☐ Very poor ☐

What points worked well? What needs developing?

How would you rate the content and structure of the presentation?

Excellent ☐ Good ☐ Average ☐ Poor ☐ Very poor ☐

What points worked well? What needs developing?

How would you rate the use of audio-visuals?

Excellent ☐ Good ☐ Average ☐ Poor ☐ Very poor ☐

What points worked well? What needs developing?

How emotionally committed to his/her subject did the presenter seem to be?

Comments:

CHAPTER 9

Balancing Your Work With the Rest of Your Life

> Here is Edward Bear, coming down stairs now, bump, bump, bump, on the back of the head, behind Christopher Robin. It is, as far as he knows, the only way of coming downstairs, but sometimes he feels that there really is another way, if only he could stop bumping for a moment and think of it.
>
> FROM WINNIE THE POOH BY A.A. MILNE

HUSBANDING YOUR RESOURCES

Robin Prior

One of the ways I've put life balance across to people is through the analogy of the milking stool. The milking stool has three legs and they represent, in your life, the work that you do, your home and love life, and your hobbies and pastimes. These three legs need to be well in place in order to have a balanced life.

Many people try to balance on one leg alone. There are many people who put all their time, energy and attention into their jobs. And then they wonder why the rest of their life doesn't work. And they also wonder why, overall, they are not happy.

There is this work ethic, a whole fallacy around commitment to a job, that unless you are giving everything of your self to the job you are not doing it properly. In fact the evidence seems to be very clear now – if you just do a sensible number of hours, with a sensible level of commitment, you live a balanced life and actually do a better job. What seems to happen is that when you restrict the number of hours that people work they use their ingenuity to find simpler ways of doing what needs to be done. They do as much but in less time, and with less negative impact on the rest of their life.

RHYTHM AND THE ART OF MANAGEMENT MAINTENANCE

> There is an old Japanese Zen story in which the master is asked the secret of his enlightenment. 'When I am hungry I eat. When I am tired I sleep,' the master enigmatically replies.

'How ordinary!' you may be thinking. But think a bit longer. Who in the world of business do you know who can put their feet up when they feel the need? At the very least it requires an office with a lock on the door and perhaps someone to hold all calls. There are the lucky few in upper management or those who work from home who can do this. Those who do it swear that it profoundly enhances their alertness, productivity and creativity.

Compare this to the energy cycles of an ordinary office. You're bright-eyed and bushy-tailed one moment. Ten minutes later, tempers are fraying with colleagues and customers, silly mistakes are made on the computer, coffee cups are tipped over documents and personal memory banks short circuit for no apparent reason. What causes these phenomena that do so much to interfere with a company's competitiveness?

Everyone is aware of the 24-hour rhythm of sleeping and waking. There are also other, shorter, rhythms of drowsiness and alertness which last from 90 minutes to two hours, known **ultradian rhythms**. Most people are vaguely aware of this shorter rhythm, one famous example being the conference mid-afternoon graveyard shift which is dreaded by so many.

Research into the body's ultradian rhythms started in the 1950s. The researchers found that the ultradian rhythms affected both mental and physical performance — concentration, memory, learning, creativity, physical co-ordination, reflexes and energy levels. It was also established that long-term interference with these rhythms was associated with a host of stress-related conditions which led to mediocre performance.

These rhythms are unconsciously recognized in the way that a standard working day is organized, for example with tea breaks in the mid-morning and mid-afternoon. This has traditionally given employees a vitally needed break in which they can refresh and rejuvenate both mind and body. However, many companies have slimmed down the size of their workforce with the result that a single employee may be doing a job that was previously covered by two or even three people. This leads to situations where employees, through a sense of guilt, fear or duty, regularly override their natural rhythms — breaks are skipped and with them the opportunity to follow the natural drowsy and rejuvenating aspect of the ultradian cycle.

REST AND REPLENISHMENT

Typically the rest part of the daily cycle either escapes our notice or is ignored. Stimulants such as sugary snacks, coffee or simply gritting the teeth are used to override our needs for rest and replenishment and put us into adrenaline overdrive. These addictive habits eventually catch up with people through health problems and/or errors in judgement.

So what are the signs and signals that can alert you to the need for an 'energy exchange'? Yawning, drowsiness, mind wandering, dreaminess, irritability, muscular tension, muscular slackness and even the need for the toilet are all signs that you are approaching the energy trough. In the best of all possible worlds you would then lie down for 20 minutes, focus on the most comfortable part of your body and let the comfort spread. But not everybody works in a sympathetic context where it is possible to take a 20-minute break. Some people will lock themselves in the toilet for five minutes and let their mind wander; others may go for walk around the block or the building or simply stand up for a stretch and a yawn. In all these cases, there is a shift down in gear from a goal-getting pace to a less hurried, process-orientated pace. It is at this point of detachment from the goal-orientated tasks that many people find the solution to problems.

This is a more naturalistic approach to stress management that, with a little practice, anybody can incorporate into the midst of their working life.

TIMING CRITICAL APPOINTMENTS TO COINCIDE WITH ULTRADIAN PEAKS

So how can you organize yourself and your staff so that you are winners in the marketplace and deliver great presentations?

1   Companies will get their money's worth from an employee who takes breaks – respect individual working rhythms as the foundations of high performance.

2   Take breaks during meetings and presentations when significant numbers of people show signs of going into energy troughs. Encourage 'spacing out' – dreaming – during breaks as a way of generating high-quality solutions to problems.

3   Wherever possible, schedule important meetings, phone calls, presentations and negotiations to coincide with high-performance energy peaks.

CHAPTER 10

Willing it and Loving it

What's money? A man is a success if he gets up in the morning and goes to bed at night and in between does what he wants to do.

Bob Dylan

If you have built castles in the air, your work need not be lost; that is where they should be. Now put the foundations under them.

Henry David Thoreau

CLOUD-WATCHING

Do you remember cloud-watching as a child? Remember the familiar and fantastic patterns that you saw there?

'There's a ship!'

'Where?'

'That group of clouds over there!'

'I still don't see a ship . . .'

'No, no. Not that group of clouds. **That** group of clouds there . . .'

'Oh yes. Now I see it. There's the bow and there's the stern . . .'

'And a huge funnel.'

'And look, those little feathery clouds could be dolphins swimming beside the ship.'

'Mmm . . . only if you screw your eyes up a little bit.'

'And look, over there, to the left . . .'

'A huge lighthouse!'

'Woahoo!'

Some people turn this ability to see patterns into a interesting skill, whether crystal ball gazing or stock market speculation. Whatever your skill, the key question is 'How can I increasingly make real more of my deepest desires, wishes and outcomes in life – personally and professionally?'

THE BIG PICTURE

All too often, however, people wait for fate or external circumstances to deal them an ace hand. Success is less a question of guessing what the future has in store for you and much more about having a hand — both hands — in creating your future.

For success as a presenter, turn to that most honest form of crystal ball — a trusted friend or colleague who listens quietly most of the time but will occasionally and yet persistently ask the probing questions that speak to the heart of the matter. Their feedback will allow you to stand back from the blinkered pursuit of goals and to survey the wider external and internal territory that is laid out before you and adjust your course accordingly.

When you are creating your own future you are ultimately dealing with something far more objective — your own subjective desires and wishes. The key question is:

What gets you up, happily and willingly, out of your bed in the morning?

. . . and what makes the process of getting out of bed a struggle and a strain?

What gives you that 'I want to' feeling . . . and what gives you that 'I have to' feeling?

You now know a lot of the techniques, beliefs and strategies for getting this to happen in presentations. Could they be applied to getting the 'want to' feeling to happen in more and more of your life?

On a very basic level if you think of the professional options that are open to you, which ones give you that 'I want to' feeling? Of course, there may be many things that you 'have to' do and many skills that you 'must' acquire to make that happen.

When considering possible future alternatives many people toss a coin. The beauty of this simple technique is that you will often find that you will be really disappointed with how the coin falls — and this in itself helps to clarify your true feelings about the course of action you truly want to take.

PLANNING YOUR LIFE

Mind you, we don't all live to work. Many people work to live and their true creative identities may be more grounded in their unpaid but highly rewarding social activities. Nonetheless the same questions hold true. What specific steps will help to bring about a much closer fit between you, the person and you, the role that you represent?

As well as considering what you want to be doing and how you are going to get sufficient skills to fulfil the role, you should consider the time scale involved. How long will it take you to get there? Six months? One year? More?

It is worth considering that a small change in one area can make all the difference to the all-round feeling of your professional and personal life.

Remember the Zen saying:

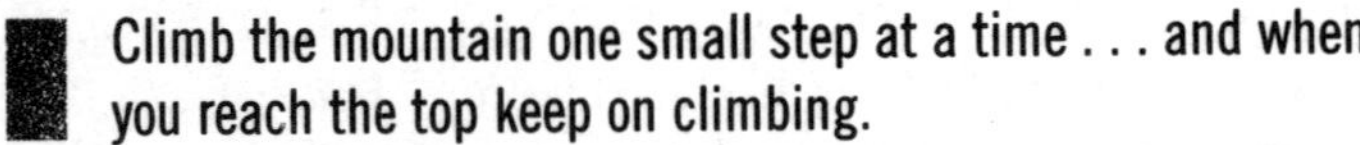

Climb the mountain one small step at a time . . . and when you reach the top keep on climbing.

NOTES

NOTES

NOTES

NOTES